TO DREAM AGAIN,

Again!

*Growing Healthy Congregations
for Changing Futures*

Robert D. Dale

Author of *To Dream Again* and *Weaving Strong Leaders*

© 2018

Published in the United States by Nurturing Faith Inc., Macon GA,
www.nurturingfaith.net.

Library of Congress Cataloging-in-Publication Data is available.

ISBN 978-1-63528-029-6

Healthy Church Resources are provided by the Center for Healthy Churches
(chchurches.org) in collaboration with Nurturing Faith Publishing
(nurturingfaith.net) and the Eula Mae and John Baugh Foundation.

Bob Dale's practical wisdom is now seasoned with decades of watching and guiding the institutional church as it finds its modern expression. Because of that, *To Dream Again* is now not only a practical guide to doing the hard work of vital congregational expression, but it also has the added richness of hard-won wisdom. And while the landscape of the church is changing radically all the time, what we know to be true about who we are called to be in our best corporate expression of God's hopes for the world is still real and true and possible. Bob Dale's voice has guided generations of congregational leaders; here he does it yet again.

—*Amy K. Butler, senior minister, Riverside Church, New York City*

Bob Dale has been dreaming for a long time. And he has been dreaming well. I have seen him dream alone, with one or two people in a hallway, in a theological classroom, in a church fellowship hall, and in conversations over a dinner meal. I guess you could say Bob Dale is a dreamer—but not in the conventional sense of mystical apparitions or hazy visions. The best way to describe Dale's style of dreaming is to use the Chinese expression for the word "dream." The Chinese translation is actually two syllables, 做梦, "make a dream." Dreaming is hard; it requires a helping verb—to make. You don't just dream—you have to make a dream. Just like Dale says, church revitalization is hard work; it requires some helping words. Ecclesiastical dreaming is not some hazy mystical vision of simple platitudes and slogans, but rather honest introspection and just plain hard work. To "make a dream" again, and maybe even again, also requires some helping people along the way willing to share their well-earned wisdom. And that is Bob Dale. Thanks for making a dream with us and for us, Bob Dale.

—*Linda McKinnish Bridges, president, Baptist Theological Seminary at Richmond*

Bob Dale offers a prophetic and creative voice to and for the church today. Theologically grounded and formed through decades of wisdom, *To Dream Again, Again!* is a wellspring of thought and practice for congregational lay leaders and clergy alike. Each section is carefully crafted, providing reflective material along with concrete facts and information gleaned from all aspects of life. Written in a conversational manner, readers are drawn in to believing they are participating in a one-to-one consultation. To assist this process, there are 13 "action exercises" drawing from the materials and applying the lived experience of the local congregation. I will be sharing this book as I pastor pastors and equip local congregations to dream!

—*Trisha M. Manarin, coordinator for mission, evangelism, and justice, Baptist World Alliance;*
executive coordinator, Mid-Atlantic Cooperative Baptist Fellowship;
director of supervised ministry, John Leland Center

I've been dreaming with Bob Dale since the '80s! He's challenged me in every aspect of my ministry. And, now he's challenging me again. Congregational vitality has to embrace change and clarity. Bob gives great insights into moving past nearsighted vision, unclarified identity, and unrealized expectations. His insights will lead you to clarify the organic purpose of your church, to dream bold dreams as you live into the next generation of your church's ministry. If you are a congregational leader, pastoral or laity, this book is for you. If you are a leader who loves your congregation and are committed to keeping your church healthy and redemptive, this book is for you. Embracing change and clarifying purpose don't have to be painful. Bob Dale challenges us to "dream again" and to be encouraged in seeing those dreams come true.

—*Bo Prosser, catalytic coach and consultant, Cooperative Baptist Fellowship*

Whatever God is saying to the church in this era of tremendous cultural change, that word is not coming from the top down—from denominational headquarters or judicatory staff. Rather, it is bubbling up from below—through the dreams of the whole people of God. Bob Dale weaves this bottom-up perspective into a revision of his classic *To Dream Again*. Building on his long commitment to congregational health and faithfulness, Dale urges us to take a more organic and Spirit-led approach to the nurture of our churches. Pastors and lay leaders alike will find much hope in these pages.

—*Jim Kitchens, principal, Pneumatrix; consultant, Center for Healthy Churches*

Few people have had the impact Bob Dale has had for me, and few books have been as influential in my life and ministry as *To Dream Again*. I celebrate that the book has been "born again." This revision and update is fresh and relevant to the 21st-century church. Bob has rewritten this classic in a way that will give it decades more of life and influence for churches and church leaders. He has a sense of what is coming, and he offers practical help for what we can do today to be ready for a world of rapid change.

—*Robert L. Perry, founder and lead consultant, Organizational Health Associates; retired pastor, missionary, and judicatory executive*

Bob Dale's book is a guiding star for church leaders navigating a journey through church renewal and rebirth. Just as Joseph, Mary, and the magi discovered the Christ child and received instruction from God through dreams, so church leaders today have the opportunity to experience God's direction. Dale retrains our clouded minds to dream wisely and practically for the challenges and ministry opportunities ahead. He provides helpful, hopeful tools to understand a congregation's natural life cycle and awakens us to new possibilities and people in our midst to begin God's new future.

—*William D. Shiell, president and professor of pastoral theology and preaching, Northern Seminary*

"Why is your church needed here and now?" That's just one of the pivotal questions Bob Dale raises in *To Dream Again, Again!* It's been my privilege to work with several congregations as they rediscovered mission and purpose with excitement and enthusiasm. Bob's *To Dream Again* provided a framework for beginning action in all of those settings. *To Dream Again, Again!*, though, provides brand new insights for times that are far more challenging than when he wrote the first book. And unlike many authors who just change a phrase here and there, Dale has recast the original in ways that provide far greater insights for current and future challenges. You won't be disappointed.

—*Bob Ballance, senior pastor, First Baptist Church, South Boston, Va.*

Contents

PART 3

Unhealthy Congregations

PART 4

Cultivating a Healthy Dream

Preface

Glancing Back, Moving Ahead

Why revise a book after more than a third of a century of steady use? For reasons both simple and complex, I'm re-visioning *To Dream Again* because . . .

- The speed of change rockets along at faster and faster rates.
- Congregational life changes, sometimes radically, often reluctantly, but always in the direction of increasing complexity.
- Leadership paradigms morph away from the machine thinking of the Industrial Age to more organic practices for living churches.
- Social media, technology, and global cultures impact local churches.
- Denominations continue to lose momentum, and institutional distrust deepens.
- American culture and churches move in different directions.
- Marketing nudges theology toward the margins in some congregations, prioritizing consumerism over faith formation.
- Gender, generations, and diversity stretch congregations in challenging ways.
- The terrorist attacks in the United States on September 11, 2001, spread fear across our culture and into our churches.
- Support for smaller and midsized churches—the majority of America's more than 420,000 congregations—continues to wane.
- New congregational styles and structures emerge.

- Fresh leadership resources and approaches have developed. Certified coaches add another type of assistance and support for leaders and congregations, alongside consultation.
- The original book, written by a 30-something, is now being reframed by a practitioner with twice the years and three times the experience.

To Dream Again (Nashville: Broadman) came out in 1981. Since then the health cycle model described in that book has provided the diagnostic framework for nearly 500 Doctor of Ministry (D.Min.) students' formal studies of congregations. The ideas and the model have shown their durability and usefulness over time.

Some elements and resources are due for an update, however. I've taken a winding road to arrive at this update:

I initially learned about organizational development from Consultant Trainers Southwest in the 1960s. Mostly an Episcopalian and Presbyterian group and part of the human potential movement, they showed me how to diagnose and renew congregations. Added to my own observations of and experiences in healthy and unhealthy churches, I began to develop my own framework for understanding congregations better.

I invested myself in teaching the emerging discipline of pastoral leadership to seminarians during the 1980s, and during that time period taught congregational diagnosis and wrote To Dream Again. Then I spent the next 20-plus years directing a learning center for pastoral and church leaders. Along the way, my teaching field expanded and my professional world morphed extensively. As I saw trends more clearly, I wrote about new approaches as they emerged.

First, I came to understand that pastoral leadership is a two-sided discipline—with mission and morale in creative tension. With that insight, I saw To Dream Again focused mostly on mission, a natural emphasis for can-do American churches and a key reason for the book's lasting popularity. To provide more leadership balance, in 1988 I wrote Keeping the Dream Alive (Nashville: Broadman), an exploration of congregational morale.

Most importantly, the biggest shift occurred in my leadership thinking when I moved from a mechanical mindset to an organic approach in the 1990s. I first wrote about this paradigm shift in Leadership for a Changing Church: Charting the Shape of the River (Nashville: Abingdon) in 1998.

That book signaled a major leadership shift in progress but not yet finished. Then in 2005 I wrote a more complete treatment of organic leadership in *Seeds for the Future: Growing Organic Leaders for Living Churches* (St. Louis: Lake Hickory Resources).

With the new leadership paradigm finally in place, I next wrote two books to clarify the practice of organic leadership. *Cultivating Perennial Churches: Your Guide to Long-Term Growth* (St. Louis: Chalice, 2008) illustrates how organic churches maintain their health and vitality over decades and even centuries. And, to explore how organic leaders adapt in rapidly changing eras, I wrote *Growing Agile Leaders: Coaching Leaders to Move with Sure-footedness in a Seismic World* (Hickory, NC: Coach Approach Ministries, 2011).

More recently Bill Wilson and I wrote *Weaving Strong Leaders: How Leaders Grow Down, Grow Up, and Grow Together* (Macon, GA: Nurturing Faith, 2016). That book returns to basics and shows how the theology and maturity of leaders make for team ministry.

Now it's time to update *To Dream Again* and consider the impacts of the bulleted changes listed earlier. Let's explore the dynamics of congregations, especially in your church. For all of us who love our churches, to understand and lead them well is part of our stewardship. This challenge will stretch us in many directions.

We'll begin with leadership practices and expand our conversation about church health from there.

Rooting Congregational Life More Deeply

We try to change congregations as organizations by three actions: (1) We change policies by adjusting the way we do things. (2) We change personnel by firing leaders, purging the ministry staff, or electing new lay leaders. (3) We tweak ministries and programs by reorganizing.

Change policy. Change people. Change programs. Each of these approaches has a host of advocates. But we recommend a fourth way to invite new seasons of congregational awakening, the most organic approach of all: We clarify purpose.

By rooting life and witness in healthy purpose, we can cultivate new life and vitality in our churches. When congregations discern and then act on their fundamental reason for being, a purposeful dream awakens and empowers them.

To Dream Again, Again! Growing Healthy Congregations for Changing Futures explores the power of congregational dreams. The health cycle model offers an organic, inside-out approach for understanding church health and avoiding pathology. To root churches in redemptive health, we'll identify and apply health cycle discoveries.

This book is for leaders, both clergy and laity, who love their congregations and are committed to keeping their churches healthy and redemptive. These leaders include:

• Ministry teams, infusing new vigor in churches of all kinds
• Congregational planners, cultivating their church's future seasons
• Church planters, seeding new congregations with healthy purpose
• Pastor selection and personnel teams, matching their congregation's dream to the leadership approach of prospective ministers
• Visionary energizers, awakening churches that are ready to dream again and regain health
• Most of all, congregational leaders, focusing, laser-like, on God's kingdom on earth

The model and principles in this book fit most volunteer (and many for-profit) organizations. Applying this model to your church is your ministry opportunity. Why? Because leaders like you are tenders of congregational health.

Ideas Germinating in Community

I owe a debt of gratitude to my "idea family" for these pages: Gayle Engels, Dave Farr, Al Persons, Eleanor Hill, Lyle Schaller, Elaine Dickson, Loren Mead, Bruce Grubbs, Ken Mitchell, Dick Hester, Larry Matthews, George Bullard, Cassidy Dale, Amy Dale, Susan McBride, Bob Perry, Phil Faig, Denny Coates, and others. Experience and discoveries from numerous church consultations have shaped my ideas too.

My appreciation also goes to Carrie Dale, Rose Mary Stewart, David Peppler, and Bob Ballance for their insightful feedback on the manuscript.

I especially thank Bill Wilson, Joel Snider, David Hull, and the consultant team at the Center for Healthy Churches for cultivating Christ's hope and health in so many congregations and for advising me on this revision.

Many other thinkers added encouragement from the sidelines. I'll take full responsibility for the words and ideas that follow, but I thank each of you for the stimulation and feedback that germinated in this revision.

The illustrations in this book represent true accounts of real church situations, with the names disguised to protect the innocent (and the guilty).

PART 1

A Model of Congregational Health

Chapter 1

Church Pulse: Values, Vision, Vitality

Church leader, ready to take your church's pulse as a baseline for its health and vitality? Use the following three cases for practice. Can you find the common theme in these true stories?

- A retired layman gives several thousand dollars each year to Crown Hills Church. On weekday mornings he frequently visits the church, dressed in work clothes, calling himself "the church gardener," and supervising the care of the lawns and shrubs. He says, "I want our church to shine as the most beautiful campus of any church in the nation!"

- After a messy fight, Old First Church splits and New Second Church forms. More than a century later the members of Old First and New Second still avoid each other. Teens from one church are forbidden to date youth from the other congregation. When a new judicatory leader accepts office space in one church's building, the other church freezes its funds for cooperative missions in the region. The judicatory leader's salary dries up.

- A growth-oriented minister accepts the pastorate at South Heights Church, a fast-growing suburban congregation. The rapid growth rate slows after a few months and finally becomes a trickle. The pastor alone feels frustrated. In a leadership meeting he accidentally overhears a remark, "We've finally arrived." When he asks about the comment, he is told (for the first time) that the founders of the church planned for a maximum membership of 700. With that number reached, the leaders are satisfied with the current size of the church. At last, the pastor realizes why he's the only one who's frustrated at the slowing growth rate.

What's the common theme in these cases? Each church holds a near-sighted view of itself. In each case there's an idea of what a church could be—but with something lacking. The Crown Hills layman wants beautiful buildings and well-groomed grounds. Both Old First and New Second see an idyllic community without the other. The South Heights leader hopes for marked growth, a view that's unnecessary to his parishioners.

What's missing? A larger redemptive vision. Vision gives churches and leaders two anchors: an identity and unique perspectives of the future.

Not all church dreams are created equal. Some congregations are founded on hope, health, and concern for others. Other congregations begin with negative and contentious attitudes. Some may be narrow in ministry and doctrine. A congregation's original dream—its identity and spirit, its sense of calling and destiny, its genetic code, its unique personality and ethos—will endure and will shape its future for a long time. DNA is destiny.

As a church leader, you want to understand your congregation better. Is it healthy? What makes it tick? Where does this health examination begin? As a first step, look for energy pools that form in a church. From that resource you'll discover what's valued and how to advance that vision and vitality.

The Power of Horizons

Healthy churches root themselves in redemptive dreams. "Captured by vision,"[1] healthy churches claim their futures. Robust dreams pave the way for significant ministries.

Think of the faith and courage it took for lay leaders to plant a Christian congregation in first-century Rome, the seat of hostile government. In Romans 16:1-16, Paul's love letter to the Roman church, Paul thanks the women and men who took huge risks and succeeded. Look at the rich roster of 24 strong leaders who launched and guided the Roman church, a church Paul never visited. For example,

- Church planters Priscilla and Aquila opened their home and hosted congregational gatherings, as they had in Corinth and Ephesus.
- Deaconess Phoebe helped set the pace of progress.
- Early convert Epaenetus contributed.
- Female twins, Tryphaena and Tryphosa, worked behind the scenes to handle hospitality.

Other names flow off the page. Their collective redemptive dream was powerful as they joined hearts and hands to plant a sturdy church in Rome.

Clear calling and vigorous leaders are key elements for healthy churches. Consider these issues as they relate to your church:

- How is your church captured by its vision?
- How is redemption central in your church's dream?
- When is it time for your church to raise its horizon?
- How ready is your church to examine its "why," its mission?
- Why is your church needed here and now?
- Why is God calling you to raise your ministry horizons and do something new?

"Why?" supplies the anchoring question wise leaders ask before undertaking new actions.[2]

With the redemptive "why?" clearly answered for your church, two other questions become timely. Your "what if?" options flow naturally when you know your "why." Finally, "how?" emerges as your implementation question.

Look at the following sequence of dream-empowering questions. Ask them, answer them, and follow them toward your dreams.[3]

1. "Why?"—to clarify calling
2. "What if?"—to generate ministry options
3. "How?"—to move ahead in redemptive practice

"Why?" provides your baseline question, raising horizons and guiding futures. Too many churches ask "how?" before they have clarified "why?" Consequently, they choose good ministries rather than essential ones. They act pragmatically before they think theologically. Then, ministry horizons lack challenge for these communities of faith.

Transformative Dreams

Dreams have impact. You and I can dream people into becoming, as Don Quixote did. His vision for people helped them develop into what he imagined for them.[4]

For weeks after I'd seen *The Man of La Mancha* on a Dallas stage, the lyric "To dream the impossible dream" lilted through my mind. Was Don Quixote the maddest man to dream impossible dreams? Or was he the sanest of men to sense the renewing power of a dream? I feel it was the latter. Don Quixote understood the "Pygmalion effect." He understood that our expectations provide springboards to real life.

Dreams best define persons and organizations. More than 80 times in the Gospels, Jesus spoke of his dream of the "kingdom of God." He dreamed of a kingdom where God rules fully in persons and over their institutions. He expected heaven to come to earth. This "kingdom dream" explains the words and works of Jesus.[5]

Jesus' dream clearly answers the identity question for any congregation, our "why." Why are we called to live out God's kingdom dream? What anchors our church?

Our ministry calling, growing as the redeemed and redeeming people of God, launches kingdom dreams in local communities and around the world. No church can minister effectively and healthily until it identifies its unique and exciting ministry dream and lives it out. We'll explore this transformative idea more in the pages that follow.

The local embodiments of Christ's kingdom dream are virtually endless. Every church, like every person, has its own personality. A church, rooted in its dream, follows its calling, utilizes its spiritual and physical resources, develops its own history, and responds to its community environment in a unique manner. But before the branches of that original dream can shape a church's life and ministry, a congregation must identify and understand the root system of its founding dream.

A Congregation's Health Cycle

How do you begin to understand another person? Likely you get to know her, observe how she acts, gather information about her goals and values to clarify your impressions, watch the interests she is pursuing, observe how she treats helpers, and then make some guesses about who she is deep inside.

The same process can help you understand an organization. Behaving, believing, becoming—track these processes and you'll discover your church's health patterns.

• How does your church act?
• What does your congregation believe?
• What growing edges does your church display?
• How does your church demonstrate its dream?
• How commonly known and deeply held is this vision by the membership at large?

Answers to these questions paint a picture of organizational life.

Humans and organizations move through a natural cycle of birth, growth, maturity, aging, and death.[6] We see this process unfold within ourselves and in organizations every day. Leaders help organizations form, reform, and transform, across a stage-by-stage arc from start-up to turn-around or decline.

This ongoing cycle depicts the dynamic and organic nature of organizational life. Churches change constantly as new ministers, different lay leaders, unique community circumstances, and fresh ministry opportunities arise. If rooted in a healthy dream, churches produce and reproduce. Or, if rootless, they become overwhelmed by their challenges, dry up, and decline toward their organizational death. Leaders of different strengths and outlooks guide congregations as they face challenges unique to each stage.

Development

Congregational health cycles display themselves clearly, as evidenced in the following steps:

1. Healthy churches are born out of a dream. They discern and **dream** a redemptive ministry. They sense and share what they feel God has called them to be and do in their setting at that moment. Then they take ownership of their vision and band together, and organizational life begins. A kingdom dream displays a congregation's soul.
2. Healthy churches **discern** and clarify their beliefs in Scripture, doctrinal statements, and music. These beliefs reveal their heart.
3. Healthy churches deliberately **choose** goals and set priorities. Goals show their logical brain.
4. Healthy churches **structure** ministries, work groups, budgets, and powerful habits (norms). Structure provides their muscles and skeleton.
5. Healthy churches **minister** out of the focused dream and trust that have developed within. Ministry puts hands and feet to their kingdom dream.

Decline

Over time, if congregations become too settled and do not take steps to invite revitalization, a plateau occurs. Doubt creeps in and decline begins, as seen in this progression:

1. With **nostalgia**, people doubt the structures: "Our church isn't working as well as it used to, is it?" Aging and atrophy set in.
2. With **questioning**, people doubt the goals: "Is this the right direction for our church?" Decline and the waning of health take root.
3. With **polarization**, people doubt the organization's basic beliefs: "This idea is wrong!" Malignancy's viral stage arrives.
4. When people become completely alienated, they **drop out** in total disillusionment: "I'm out of here!" Hospice for human spirits now sits in the pews. Absolute doubt marks the death of the kingdom dream in these persons in this place.

Now you have a picture of your church's organizational life. Can you locate your congregation on this cycle? Does it lean more toward the healthy or unhealthy side?

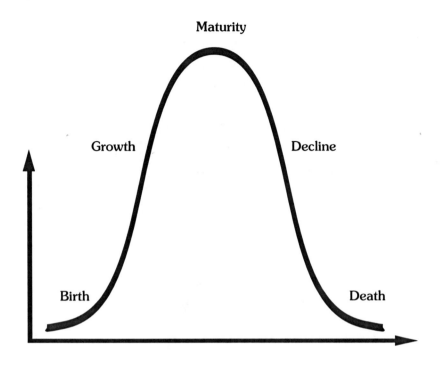

♦♦♦

Organizationally speaking, healthy churches *focus on possibilities.* They pursue their vision and welcome their futures, show energy and take ministry initiatives, build on and are renewed by their dream, and minister to others.

In comparison, unhealthy churches *center on problems,* reactively and unhealthily obsessed with defending the present. They descend into doldrums and lose momentum for ministry, doubt themselves into decline and death, and need ministry for their own survival.

I call this model "the health cycle." Savvy leaders learn how to take the pulse of their congregation and understand its health cycle. This book focuses on how you can be God's partner in developing and maintaining organizational health in your church. You'll explore each health cycle stage. As importantly, you'll learn how to help your church dream again!

Leadership Applications

What leadership actions from the health cycle model guide your church and its ministry? Consider these suggestions:

• Healthy churches constantly **cultivate revitalization**. They dream and dream again. To stand still invites death. Worship, study, and fellowship offer regular opportunities for individual and corporate refreshment. Healthy churches steadfastly stay rooted in their theological dream.

• Leaders, often clergy, help congregations **keep their dream clear**. They help develop new approaches to understanding "why we're here," "who we are," and "what we're working together to be and do." They gather to choose and cultivate dream-based futures. They build morale by harnessing the energy and hope generated by new dreams.

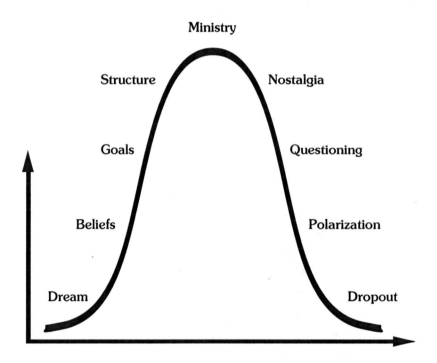

• Dreaming churches **plant seeds and plan for tomorrow**; doubting churches get mired down in solving today's problems. Regular seasons of discerning and refocusing on dreams energize congregations, keeping both their roots and horizons clear to their members.

• Healthy churches **replant and nurture their dreams**, not their doubts. Organizational structures exist to implement and extend the dream.

(A friendly warning may be appropriate for ministers new to a church: During honeymoon periods resist the temptation to restructure; understand your church's dream first.)

- Healthy churches **commit primarily to their dream-goals** and only secondarily to their programs and structures, pruning ministries too weak to extend the dream and planting new ministries refreshed by the dream. The power of redreaming provides better launch points for organizational health than reprogramming or restructuring.

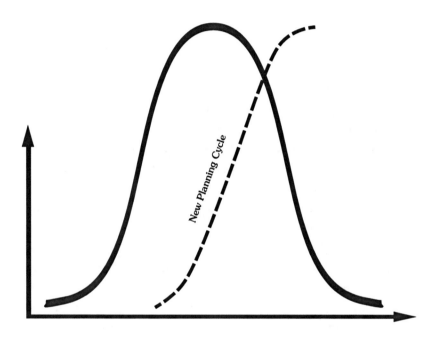

New Planning Cycle

- Healthy churches **monitor their vitality**. Churches that slide below the questioning stage on the health cycle put themselves in grave danger. Doubt opens the door to decline and perhaps organizational death. Questioning is, organizationally speaking, the point of no return. Remember: God can transform and redeem any situation. But, humanly speaking, we can't bring life to near-dead organizations by our own efforts.

- Healthy dreams **anchor healthy organizations**. Nothing less than a kingdom dream will turn churches toward healthy and effective ministry.

• A planning cycle rooted firmly in the dream **aids organizational health**. Each cycle renews and stretches the organization to new heights. Kingdom ministry thrives on dream planning.

Organizations contain the seeds for their own lives and of their own deaths. Even congregations founded on healthy dreams can drift into destructive patterns. When healthy organizations sense their decline, they begin to dream again. This life-or-death choice invites new futures.

Your Church's Health

The health cycle model, like a medical exam for your church, detects its vital signs. Take a step toward health by raising key questions:

• What health stage describes our church now?
• What characterizes our health at this stage?
• What health challenges and transitions await us?
• What leadership strengths can move us beyond this health stage?
• What preparation readies us for the next stages in our health cycle?

Apply the health cycle model to your congregation by using the action-reflection exercises scattered throughout this book. Consider carefully the basic ideas in the first two chapters. Then, you'll know much more about your church's health. You'll also be able to assess the health status of other congregations quickly.

As a first step, use the model in *To Dream Again, Again!* as a guide to your church's health. Let's now move to the model and its applications.

Notes

[1]George W. Bullard, *Captured by Vision* (Nashville: Westbow, 2017).

[2]Simon Sinek, *Start with Why: How Great Leaders Inspire Everyone to Take Action* (New York: Portfolio/Penguin, 2009).

[3]Warren Berger, *A More Beautiful Question: The Power of Inquiry to Spark Breakthrough Ideas* (New York: Bloomsbury, 2014).

[4]Portions of the following material are adapted from my original article "To Dream a Possible Dream," *Search*, Summer 1978, 35-38.

[5]C. L. Mitton makes this almost universally accepted point in *The Good News* (New York: Abingdon, 1961), 71-79

⁶This *provolutionary* (a Latin word meaning "to turn toward the future") model was developed originally by Management Designs, Inc. of Cincinnati, Ohio, for the United Church of Christ. Published in a consultant's resource book titled *Strengthening the Local Church* (New York: Council for Lay Life & Work, 1974), this model was designed as a process to revitalize congregations. I've adapted the terms in the initial model, but have retained and extended most of the basic provolutionary concepts of organizational life. The life cycle format has classically been applied to organizational phenomena. Several examples illustrate the life cycle school of thought: Gordon L. Lippitt, in *Organizational Renewal* (New York: Meredith, 1969), 29, depicts the "developmental stages of organizational growth" as birth, youth, and maturity. Paul Hersey and Kenneth H. Blanchard, in *Management of Organizational Behavior*, 3ʳᵈ ed. (Englewood Cliffs, NJ: Prentice-Hall, 1977), 299-302, describe organizational growth as a series of evolution (stable growth)-revolution (crisis) stages. E. Mansel Pattison, in *Pastor & Parish—A Systems Approach* (Philadelphia: Fortress, 1977), 57-69, applies developmental stages to the church and claims that a social system matures as it moves from storming to forming to norming to performing. Louis A. Allen Associates, an international business consulting firm, advertises in their brochures that companies experience an adolescent stage between infancy and maturity. They term this crucial stage "the corridor of crisis" and depict it as a make-or-break organizational stage. They note, remarkably, of the 20 largest companies in the United States after World War II, only two are still among the first 20 in size. Of the 100 largest companies at the end of the 20ᵗʰ century, almost half have disappeared or have declined substantially from their peak. Further information on the management system the Allen Associates has developed is available from 615 University Ave., Palo Alto, CA 94301. Organizations either renew or die. All kinds of organizations wax or wane. David O. Moberg, in *The Church as a Social Institution* (Englewood Cliffs, NJ: Prentice-Hall, 1962), 118-124, applies a life cycle approach to denominations. For additional information, see LeRoy Thompson Jr., in *Mastering the Challenges of Change: Strategies for Each Stage in Your Organization's Life Cycle* (New York: AMACOM, 1994) Life cycle models continue to be developed and used by churches. See Tony Morgan, *The Unstuck Church: Equipping Churches to Experience Sustained Growth* (Nashville: Thomas Nelson, 2017).

Chapter 2

Church Health: Vital Signs for Living Communities

Imagine you're in your medical doctor's office for your annual check-up. He asks about your health concerns, looks at your test results, takes your blood pressure, listens to your heart and lungs, and orders other exams as needed. He looks at your vital signs to understand your current and future health better.

If you listened to the heart and inner workings of healthy congregations, you would hear the pulsations of at least four vital signs:

1. An organic theology for living communities of faith
2. An appreciation for the multiplier role of leaders
3. An awareness of how congregations are unique organizations
4. The roles leaders fill as spiritual health professionals

Let's explore these health indicators and create a medical chart for the life of your congregation.

Theological Roots

Ready to plant some theology-of-practice seeds?[1] In organic fashion, Scripture describes the church in living images. Bodies and vines, plants and harvests, gardens and growth abound.

The church of Jesus Christ lives. Unlike machines, faithful congregations are eternally changing, learning, discerning, exploring, and maturing. In healthy churches, signs of organic life and liveliness surround us. As leaders of living churches, we plant, feed, cultivate, weed, prune, and harvest. Then, observing the rhythms of seasons, we repeat the growth process again and again.

By giving attention to these organic images from Scripture, we can cultivate deep roots for congregational life. Roots are vital, providing two essential functions for plants: They give stability and reach out for life-giving nourishment.

Look at the following ways roots stabilized and nourished churches in the New Testament.

The Body of Christ

The body of Christ, an image of life and liveliness, stands central in Paul's writings. Writing to the church in Corinth, Paul described the "body of Christ" in tangible, organic terms (1 Cor. 12:12-31). With Christ as head, the body of Christ made up of diverse parts remains unified. Each member of the body contributes uniquely, yet all are interdependent.

Paul points to feet and hands, ears and eyes, all different, yet all essential to the body. Every part of the body is honored and needed. Joy and suffering are shared mutually by the body. Connections within the body of Christ call us to respect and support each other. Being one, our relationships remain faithful to Christ's body.

Organic theology roots the visible church. In the past, churches reflected the machine-like approaches from our traditions and denominations. In the 21st century we cultivate an organic, missional theology of the visible church.[2]

Historically, theologians spoke more of the mystical "bride of Christ" than the tangible, organic "body of Christ." In the past, theologians explained ecclesiology more fully than on the gathered fellowship's mission in the world. Still, some Protestant thinkers explored the visible church powerfully. Karl Barth asserted, "The first congregation was a visible group, which caused a visible public uproar. If the Church has not this visibility, then it is not the Church."[3]

Organic theology focuses congregational relationships on their mission within their context. Scripture's earliest churches—communities of fellowship, prayer, and outreach—showed a clear purpose for being. They acted with passion on their kingdom calling. If formerly we focused more on methodology and machinery than theology and health, we now seize our opportunity to recover our theological and relational roots within the body of Christ.

Vine and Branches

John 15 points out the distinctive roles of organic theology's leaders. In this powerful passage clear roles define relationships: God owns the vineyard, Jesus depicts the vine, and faithful believers provide the branches. The branches produce fruit naturally. The vinedresser knows and practices a gardening truth: fruit only grows on new wood. So, at the end of each season, dead wood is pruned away to stimulate new production on new wood in the next growing season.

In a mechanical world, non-production is met with tuning and tweaking. But in an organic universe those branches, no longer producing fruit, feel the keen edge of pruning shears and get discarded.

My grandfather had an apple orchard. As a child, I thought it was fun to pick apples during the harvest season. But I also remember it was both thrilling and ominous for me to watch the fall bonfire as deadwood met its fate. Produce or be pruned: that's the cautionary tale of organic growth processes.

"Soul growth"[4] spurs organic health in our congregations. New vitality, then, leads to new harvests.

Planting and Harvesting

The parable of the sower and the soils depicts readiness for growth in organic terms (Matt. 13:1-23, Mark 4:1-20, Luke 11:21-22). This story describes both the generosity of the sower and the receptivity of the soil. In classic storytelling form the seeds are broadcast on three kinds of soils, with only one ready to produce a crop.

God's work of germination and growth partners with the soils in this story. The evil one's work dooms some seeds to death. Even so, three magnitudes of yields—all impressive—bless the harvest.

Gardeners, savvy about sowing good seeds, prepare soils with good angles to the sun and tend their plants. Receptivity for growth always combines organic factors.

Gardens and Grace

In Scripture, gardens stimulate growth and renewal, each in season. Winter's chill falls on Eden's garden when Adam and Eve turn away from their destinies (Genesis 13). Spring's potential arises in Gethsemane's garden, where God's will completely orients Jesus' life and ministry (Matt. 26:36-46, Mark 13:32-42, Luke 22:40-46). Summer's hope arrives when Jesus rises from Golgotha's garden tomb (John 19:41). And, fall's harvest triumph will finally emerge when the faithful gather around the tree of life in God's heavenly garden (Rev. 2:7).

Organic leaders recognize that life moves through seasons of reproduction and rest naturally and perpetually. We prepare our congregations for the opportunities, paces, and challenges of each season.

Now, with deep roots for our churches, let's focus on leaders.

Multiplier Leaders

Today's lively organic approach to organizational life and leadership stands in stark contrast to the static machine images of the older Industrial Age.[5] Mechanical leaders assumed that organizations could be started, stopped, tuned, and junked. This model saturated Western culture and left marks on the structures and operations of American denominations.

This machine pattern remains familiar in established churches, since many Protestant groups developed amid the heyday of the Industrial Age. The machine legacy receded rapidly in the 21st century as the speed of change and need for agility in leaders increased. The era of congregations as "well-oiled machines," never a realistic expectation, is now dying away.

Look at current examples from three frontline leadership arenas—business, military, and religious organizations—as they continue to morph toward organic approaches. Traditionally, leadership in the public sector built on models from business and the military. In the service sector, church and not-for-profit leaders mostly copied and pasted from the public sector.

Business World

In the business world traditional industrial leaders built pyramidal structures, bossed subordinates, and invented mass production. Traditional bureaucratic approaches embedded themselves in the lives of local churches as leaders, mostly laity, imported practices from the business world. Organic leaders of the 21st century create "flatter" business organizations, share responsibilities in partnerships with employees, and expand entrepreneurial networks.[6]

Churches need management, but their callings are beyond business practices alone.

Military Arena

In the military the older styles of leadership and organization, also highly structured, made commanders into bureaucrats in uniforms. Troops were regimented, fought in lines, and waited on orders. As Tom Ricks in *The Generals* described clearly, America's military fought well and won in World War II, but not afterward. Why? We lost our ability to adapt against newer guerrilla-style enemies who don't stand and fight. Our new military, moving toward more flexibility and agility in its Special Operations forces, disperses authority across units to make immediate decisions under fire.[7]

Churches face conflicts, but they need the military's adaptability and agility too.

Religious Organizations

After three or four centuries of mechanistic practices, new practices are emerging in American churches. Look at these changes: disappearance of one-size-fits-all programs, paring down of structures, shortening of time needed to make congregational decisions, and increasing missional focus. As living communities, churches adapt—unlike inanimate machines.

More agility in church leaders increases their effectiveness.

Organic leaders see multiplication as their unique call. Especially in congregational settings, they magnify potential.[8] Multiplier leaders spread health virally. They . . .

• See the gifts of others and amplify those gifts.
• Start connecting conversations, ask questions, and listen.
• Create settings in which teams can imagine and innovate.
• Expect the best from themselves and from those around them.
• Exercise perspective and show humor.
• Do not demand to be the smartest or most controlling persons in the room.

Multipliers lead for the sake of God's kingdom in the living churches they serve. They live in a new world that calls for unique difference-makers.

Congregational Distinctiveness

As we have described, churches are one-of-a-kind organizations. From an organizational perspective, what distinctive roles do congregations demonstrate publicly to the world? Consider these:

• Congregations are **living** organizations. Never inanimate machines, they thrive by planting, nurturing, and harvesting—the basic life processes in churches.

• Congregations are **missional** organizations. They exist to extend the kingdom of God, the redemptive dream of Jesus. The church calls persons to live by distinctly Christian values; to incarnate Jesus' kingdom dream, a prophetic role of the church.

• Congregations are **molding** organizations. Molding lives challenges any group hoping to exercise religious or cultural or social influence. Standing as contrast communities, congregations incarnate a new model: the Christ life. Congregations shape the lives and consciences of our own members and our communities. Churches take risks to shape the future, because our ultimate future stands secure.

• Congregations are **volunteer** organizations. To be effective, volunteer groups can ask and answer four basic questions with imagination. These key questions define the participatory role of the church in the larger world.

1. What's our mission?

"Why?" is the most fundamental question a volunteer organization can ask itself.[9] Businesses say, "Our purpose is to make a profit," or "We exist to sell one warehouse full of widgets every month." The church, however, deals in redemptive relationships, connections of persons to God and of persons to others. These relational measures, much more difficult to see, matter most. As a result, congregations can't risk defining their mission in vague generalities or not at all. With eternity at risk, congregations constantly discern and sharpen their reason for being.

2. How does our church pay its volunteers?

Volunteers work together to create a distinctive style of organization. There are no paychecks or fringe benefits for volunteers. Rather, volunteers take their "pay" in spiritual or psychological gains. Think of gains in service, recognition, learning, ministry channels, and moral ways to fill time and to structure life. With no gains, volunteers "un-volunteer," no longer contributing time and energy. Therefore, congregations, when crystal-clear about volunteers' benefits, contribute more to God's kingdom.

3. How unique are we in a world crowded with other volunteer organizations?

Congregations live in a competitive world, sometime naively. For instance, a rural community in eastern North Carolina with 1,100 residents counted its volunteer organizations. It discovered 83 formally organized groups, including 7 churches. That's 75 volunteer organizations for every 1,000 persons in the community! When informed of these statistics, a longtime resident replied: "I thought it would be closer to a thousand. It sometimes seems we have more organizations than people around here."[10] As volunteer organizations, churches compete for peoples' allegiance with youth sports leagues, 4-H, Scouts, Weight Watchers, garden clubs, and PTA. Therefore, congregations must calculate how much time they can expect from members. Religiously, God demands all. Organizationally, churches often must settle for less time and contribution from their membership.

4. How does the health of our church measure up?

Volunteer organizations, the most complex and sophisticated organizational form humans know, challenge leaders. Volunteer organizations do not coerce their members. Either church members receive "pay" for their volunteer energy, or they drop out. People join volunteer groups for motivations other than wages. These characteristics make volunteer groups challenging to understand and the most difficult to lead.

With only two organizational climates, healthy and unhealthy, it's paramount that congregations develop and maintain organizational health. The health cycle model gives church leaders a concrete method for understanding key issues in organizational health.

Health Ministers

Ministers wear many hats as we serve church health. We traditionally have preached, taught, led worship, provided pastoral care, and done evangelism. The newest roles to emerge in pastoral ministries revolve around leadership, management, and organizational development.

The ministry of congregational health calls on church leaders to nourish and cultivate the body of Christ. Organizational development in the church places some new, but necessary, challenges on ministers and church lay leaders—somewhat akin to those faced by health care professionals.

Preventive Medicine

Ministers, as internal coaches and consultants, guide their congregations toward health. This crucial helping ministry enables congregations to discover their unique personality, offset their limitations, and seize their current and future opportunities. As family physicians for congregations, ministers diagnose, design, and facilitate processes that discern and define the kingdom dream, moving the body of believers toward health.[11]

Specifically, the "action exercises" in this book provide clue questions and frameworks for developing a complete profile of congregational health. The information gathered through the action exercises can provide a diagnosis of your church. Consider the action exercises as your health laboratory, your path to a congregational self-study.

Church Diagnosis

"Reading" congregations is a crucial ministry skill.[12] The health cycle model offers a series of diagnostic stages for congregational analysis, diagnosis, and revitalization. By using this model, leaders can determine the current stage of their church, isolate key health issues, and treat maladies constructively and proactively so as to restore vitality and renewal.

For example, let's assume your congregation is in the nostalgia stage of health. That's your discovery through analysis. What do you do, then, to awaken new vitality in the total organization? Consider these possibilities:

- Look directly across the model for the organizational sticking point. Nostalgia doubts structure, pinpointing nostalgia's trouble spot. A common mistake at this point involves simple restructuring, which is generally too cosmetic and helps only briefly.

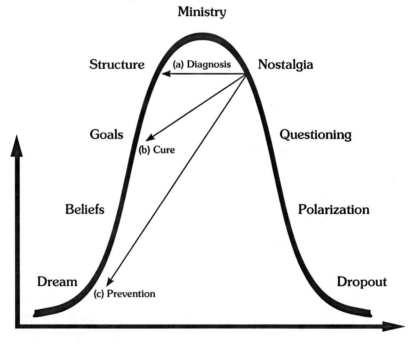

- Since structure grows out of organizational goals, find the cure in an examination of the goals. Determine how the goals and structure mesh and if new or different goals have left the structure largely outmoded.

• Preventive organizational medicine calls us to return to a sharpened, owned, and communicated kingdom dream. The dream contains the spiritual and emotional motivation to launch a congregation on a new cycle of redemptive ministry.

Health Planning

Ministers serve as visionary leaders, unleashing the prophetic energy and sense of group power in the dream while also using resources wisely. Planning, a pivotal skill for leaders, blends the art of the visionary and the science of resource management. Ministers, who hope to serve as effective leaders and growth agents, will develop planning as a vehicle for congregational effectiveness. With a kingdom dream as the seedbed for church health, planning from that dream can cultivate healthy growth.

◆◆◆

We've explored four roles that leaders play in developing and enhancing congregational health. These are our vital signs.

Vital Signs in Action

With your congregation's "medical chart" open, you're ready to explore the four vital signs of living communities—theological roots, multiplier leaders, congregational distinctiveness, and health ministers—and locate your church on the health cycle model. There's much to do as you dream and plan. Move ahead with faith, hope, and love.

Too often we in the church have been handed programs by our own denominations or by outside experts. Less often have we been helped to see why our churches exist or why we minister to others. This book focuses on why we dream of God's redemption and how to develop healthy congregations.

To our earlier model of congregational health, stir together the four vital signs related to organic theology, leader roles, organizational types, and health functions. Using these foundations, let's look in detail at the process of triggering congregational health by dreaming again.

As you read and think about your church's health, consider two applications: (1) Use *To Dream Again, Again!* as a do-it-yourself project to strengthen the vitality of your church and to help you understand your church better and serve as a more effective multiplier leader. (2) If you discover issues that are bigger and deeper than you can resolve, call on a reliable consultant to help your membership become healthier.[13]

Notes

[1]Robert D. Dale, *Seeds for the Future: Growing Organic Leaders for Living Churches* (St. Louis: Lake Hickory Resources, 2005).

[2]Stanley J. Grenz, *Theology for the Community of God* (Nashville: Broadman & Holman, 1994), 657.

[3]Karl Barth, *Dogmatics in Outline* (New York: Harper & Row, 1959), 142.

[4]Terry Hershey, *Soul Gardening* (Minneapolis: Augsburg, 2002).

[5]Peter M. Senge, "Leadership in Living Organizations" in Frances Hesselbein, Marshall Goldsmith, and Iain Somerville, *Leading Beyond the Walls* (San Francisco: Jossey-Bass, 1994), 73-90.

[6]Peter Drucker, *Management: Tasks, Responsibilities, Practices* (New York: Harper & Row, 1974), 74-94. While this chapter focuses on "business purpose and business mission," the issue is so basic to organizational health and effectiveness that church leaders apply this concept to congregational life.

[7]Thomas E. Ricks, *The Generals: Military Command from World War II to Today* (New York: Penguin, 2012).

[8]Liz Wiseman, *Multipliers: How the Best Leaders Make Everyone Smarter* (New York: HarperCollins, 2010).

[9]Lyle E. Schaller, *The Pastor and the People* (Nashville: Abingdon, 1973), 80-86.

[10]Lyle E. Schaller, *Understanding Tomorrow* (Nashville: Abingdon, 1976), 96-97.

[11]To help leaders and ministers understand the consultant role when groups explore the future together, see: Annette Simmons, *A Safe Place for Dangerous Truths* (New York: AMACOM, 1999); Edgar H. Schein, *Process Consultation* (Reading, MA: Addison-Wesley, 1969); Robert R. Blake and Jane Srygley Mouton, *Consultation* (Reading, MA: Addison-Wesley, 1976); and Walter H. Mahler, *Diagnostic Studies* (Reading, MA; Addison-Wesley, 1974).

[12]To discover and build on group strengths, see Jane Magruder Watkins and Bernard J. Mohr, *Appreciative Inquiry: Change at the Speed of Imagination* (San Francisco: Jossey-Bass/Pfeiffer, 2001). Also see Seymour L. Rosenberg, *Self-Analysis of Your Organization* (New York: AMACOM, 1974); Jack K. Fordyce and Raymond Weil, *Managing with People* (Reading, MA: Addison-Wesley, 1971); Mahler, *Diagnostic Studies*; and Marvin R. Weisbord, "Organizational Diagnosis: Six Places to Look for Trouble with or without a Theory" in *Group and Organization Studies*, December 1976, 430-447.

[13]To see what quality congregational consulting provides, check the resources and approaches of the Center for Healthy Churches at www.chchurches.org.

PART 2

Healthy
Congregations

Chapter 3

Christ's Kingdom: A Redemptive Dream

The famous African-American poet Langston Hughes grasped the power of a life vision: "Hold fast to dreams, for if dreams die, life is a broken winged bird that cannot fly."

Healthy churches dream about God's kingdom in similar ways. Unhealthy churches live out their own distinctive nightmares. Churches are born, mature, and stay vital out of a dream. This redemptive dream is the soul of our healthy churches.

What is the source of redemptive visions for churches? To propel church health, look toward two basic spiritual life sources: biblical teachings about redemption and deliberate congregational discernment. These two sources often flow together into unity around a church's dream. Dreams, seen with our heart, lead us toward and beyond our horizons.

Clarifying Your Personal Dream

We who lead help our churches dream their dreams. Therefore, we too must live from a clear personal dream.

Arthur Miller's classic *Death of a Salesman* spotlights the cost of a wrong dream. Willie Loman, a born craftsman, fashioned the front stoop of his house. But Willie tried instead to become a super salesman. When his sales dropped, he snapped under the strain and killed himself. Biff, Willie's son, stood by his father's grave and said, "There's more of him in that front stoop than in all the sales he ever made. He had the wrong dreams. All, all wrong."[1]

Jesus dreamed rightly of God's kingdom. He taught and lived his vision, typical of many young adults. Jesus' kingdom dream organized and motivated his life. Daniel Levinson, after extensive study of developmental patterns, says the dream in young adults is "more formed than pure fantasy, yet less articulated than a fully thought-out plan." Furthermore, the dream "has the quality of a vision, and imagined possibility that generates excitement and vitality."[2] To understand and follow Jesus, grasping his dream of the kingdom of God becomes job number one for leaders.

Jesus' ministry dream calls us—we believers will live the reign of God on earth as it is in heaven. That vision transforms us and our world, according to Gregory Boyd: "God's dream has always been for humans to form a single, united community under his loving Lordship."[3]

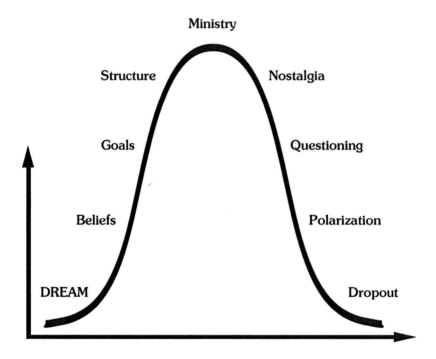

A first step in awakening a kingdom dream in a congregation happens when key leaders search for their personal dreams. Why? Because personal dreams often bloom into organization-wide dreams. As Ralph Waldo Emerson famously said, "An institution is but the lengthened shadow of a man (or woman)."

Following is a checklist to help you clarify your own dream. With this and other action exercises in this book, I would suggest using this approach:

• Reflect on your own clue questions. Use your knowledge and impressions of your congregation to deepen and broaden your individual perspective.

• Talk to others informally, using the clue questions to deepen and widen your view of your church.

• Or, alternatively, enlist a formal self-study team of church members, varied by gender, age, commitment levels, lengths of membership, and levels of activity. A planning committee or leadership council can serve as a "vitality group" to consult with and to make discoveries together.

ACTION EXERCISE #1
Personal Ministry Inventory

What's your dream for your own ministry? Leaders imagine, sense opportunities, identify real needs, make calculated guesses about the future's possibilities, put ideas into practical plans, and call persons to kingdom service. Ministerial leaders serve as visionary stewards of congregational opportunities and resources. Here's a checklist for outlining a visionary ministry for yourself:

• What *kind of Christians* do I dream of?
• What *kind of ministries* can I develop to grow my dream Christians?
• What *kind of leadership team* of volunteer and/or paid staff can I develop to produce my dream church ministries?
• What *kind of minister leader* can I become to gather my dream leadership team?
• What *kind of support system* of family, peers, and friends do I need to help me become the leader I dream of?
• What *kind of new world* is created by my kingdom dream?

In the words of the sage, "Where there is no vision, the people perish" (Prov. 29:18). But where there's a kingdom dream, God's people flourish.

Peoples' dreams define their lives to a large extent. William Herbert Carruth's poem, "Dreamer of Dreams," shows how the rise and fall of personal dreams shape our lives.[4]

We are all of us dreamers of dreams,
On visions our childhood is fed;
And the heart of the child is unhaunted, it seems,
By the ghosts of dreams that are dead.
From childhood to youth's but a span
And the years of our life are soon sped;
But the youth is no longer a youth, but a man,
When the first of his dreams is dead.
…
He may live on by compact and plan
When the fine bloom of living is shed,
But God pity the little that's left of a man
When the last of his dreams is dead.
Let him show a brave face if he can,
Let him woo fame or fortune instead,
Yet there's not much to do but bury a man
When the last of his dreams is dead.

Without a dream, we have no direction in life. Dreams give us a story to tell and a reason to live. Organizations dream too.

Congregational dreams launch from their members' vision of life. Two experts on developing organizations note that "at its inception, any organization is an expression of the purposes of its individual founders."[5] So, organizations develop their stories and tell them repeatedly, transmitting them to all who will listen.

Retelling Kingdom Stories

Jesus came telling stories. Parables formed the core of his teaching. Many of his parables begin, "The kingdom of God is like . . ." These 50-60 kingdom stories in the Gospels make up about 35 percent of Jesus' teachings.[6] More than 80 times in the Gospels Jesus spoke of the kingdom of God (or the kingdom of heaven in Matthew). Virtually all of his parables centered on the kingdom vision. These kingdom stories can awaken personal and congregational dreams as we listen with our soul.

Clear Communication

Kingdom stories communicate easily. Jesus' parables provide vocabularies for our common narratives. For example, when persons become obvious rebels or sinners, they earn the "prodigal" description (Luke 15:11-24).

The parables paint word pictures. They compare and contrast the full range of life experience. Some kingdom stories capture one-frame images, akin to proverbs (Mark 3:24). Others read like short films, depicting brief stories such as the Good Samaritan (Luke 10:25-37).

The communication factor helps visionary leaders express a redemptive dream through retelling Jesus' kingdom stories.

What Gospel story calls you? How do you tell it?

Exciting Lessons

Kingdom stories make learning exciting. Discovering and acting on your dream electrifies you. With more to learn always, we remain rookies and pioneers in God's kingdom. Our faith journey continues to unfold across our entire life span.

A parable's educational factor depends on its capacity to stimulate thinking. It acts like a headlight's reflector, focusing illumination on its subject and concentrating on a single truth about God's kingdom.

Vivid Pictures

Kingdom stories paint vivid pictures for us. Parables engage our imagination. Their impact turns our ears into eyes, helping us "see" what we hear. These stories, originally and currently, remain so unforgettable that they are the purest form of Jesus' teachings we have. We are drawn to the parables and act on them, because we see the insights and actions they teach.

The kingdom stories contain a motivation factor that energizes us to respond to kingdom dreams. Our dreams move us forward.

Jesus' kingdom stories make his kingdom dream concrete. Healthy congregations dream of a visible kingdom and work to live out their dreams concretely and to bring heaven to earth. Then, those focused communities tell and retell their stories. Teaching the parables stretch us to consider kingdom dreams for ourselves.

Defining Your Congregation's Kingdom Dream

Outsiders can't define your congregation's kingdom dream. I don't know the special needs and ministry opportunities beckoning to your congregation. I don't see how God moves in your midst. But some foundational themes provide bases for your unique congregational expression of the kingdom of God. Build on these themes.

Redemption

Kingdom dreams begin with redemption. God's consistent purpose has always been to redeem his creatures and creation. Redemption sums up the Bible's story in a single word.

The parables strongly extend the theme of redemptive grace. The two debtors (Luke 7:36-50), the lost sheep and lost coin (Luke 15:1-10), the waiting father / prodigal son (Luke 15:11-32), and the unforgiving debtor (Matt. 18:23-35) all tell of God's mercy toward sinners. Repenting and believing provide pre-conditions for persons who give themselves to God's kingdom.

Redeeming persons and their institutions defines basic kingdom ministry for congregations. Without redemption as their baseline, churches become social clubs or short-term helping agencies. Redemption always forms the foundations for kingdom dreams.

God's Ruling

Kingdom dreams envision God ruling. God leads, and we follow our king in humble obedience. Our highest value remains living humbly as citizens under the rule of God's kingdom.

Again, Jesus' parables speak of sacrificing for kingdom participation. God rules actively and continuously; the kingdom citizen responds readily and joyfully. The tower builder and the warring king (Luke 14:28-33), the hidden treasure and precious pearl (Matt. 13:44-46), the unresponsive neighbor and the callous judge (Luke 11:5-8, 18:2-8), the farmer and his helper (Luke 17:7-10), and the two builders (Matt. 7:24-27)—all of these call on men and women of the kingdom to hear God's ruling commands and to do his bidding.

Doing the will of God remains the individual Christian's highest goal. Beyond individual members of congregations, however, the kingdom of God demands a corporate commitment to God's will. Congregations seek for and pledge themselves to act, as a body, on the instructions of a ruling God. Christ-centered ministry flows from a church's kingdom dream.

Christ's Concreteness

Kingdom dreams make Christ concrete. Jesus incarnated the kingdom of God. Beyond teaching, Jesus acted out some of his lessons. The triumphal entry, the cleansing of the temple, and the Lord's Supper describe enacted lessons or embodied parables.

Jesus came preaching the gospel of the kingdom. Not adhering to an abstract theory, he lived the kingdom practically. Christian disciples and congregations embody the kingdom of God every day in every generation. When kingdom dreams become tangible in a congregation's ministry, heaven comes to earth.

Growth and Change

Kingdom dreams trigger growth and change. God's kingdom changes people and their institutions. God's imagination is unlimited, but worlds need to expand. The theme of growth runs throughout the parables. The sower (Mark 4:3-8), the seed growing secretly (Mark 4:26-29), the mustard seed and leaven (Luke 13:18-21, Mark 4:30-32), the weeds among the wheat

(Matt. 13:24-30), and the kernel of wheat (John 12:24) make growth and change constants in the kingdom.

For persons and congregations to develop a dynamic kingdom dream, they willingly accept the risks of growing into their hopes.

With these theological foundations, let's look at your church's dream.

Discovering Your Congregation's Founding Dreams

Do you know the original dream of your congregation? Unearthing the founding dream of your church may take some careful analysis and a bit of imagination. Discovering beginnings, especially when your church is older, can be challenging. If many years have elapsed, original members have died, and poor records have been kept, you may not fully discover your church's founding dream.

Nevertheless, the originating dream is likely woven into both the past history and the current behavior patterns of your congregation. Delving into both can help you develop enough understanding to dream again.

Some facets of the dream will be obvious. For example, after a bitter division in the Without Spot or Blemish Church, some dissident members withdrew and established a rival church directly across the street. They named the new congregation The Greater Without Spot or Blemish Church! The name tells the tale.

One school of social psychiatry teaches that our lives have an element of predictability, as if we are living out of a playwright's script. Finding and reading our "script" helps us understand and cope with some of the patterns of our lives.

Organizations have scripts or stories too.[7] Your church, shaped by its behavior, dream, history, and decisions, tells its story automatically. Persons and churches, quickly becoming creatures of habit, live out past patterns in ways seen and unseen.

How would you have responded to a challenge from the California Gold Rush of 1849? As the wagon trains left Saint Joseph, Missouri for the trek across western prairies already rutted by the tracks of earlier wagons, eager pioneers read this sobering message on a banner across the western end of Main Street: "Choose your rut carefully. You may be in it all the way to California!" Discovering your church's ruts can help you understand visible and invisible determinants of your faith community's direction.

The following informal script questionnaire can aid in diagnosing your church's predictable patterns. Then, if you find routines that run counter to kingdom dreams, you can challenge and change them. With the help of this questionnaire, some historical information, and careful observation of your church's current behavior, you can clarify the scripted dream of your congregation.

ACTION EXERCISE #2
A Script Questionnaire for Our Church

ACT I: The Early Days
- Who was our church's founder, earliest leaders, first pastor, and charter members? How would you describe these persons?
- How was our church born: out of positive or negative circumstances?
- What do the earliest records of our church say about our church's beginning?
- What projects did our church undertake first?
- Does our church's constitution, bylaws, or legal documents contain unique or unusual features? Do they speak for or against certain themes that indicate the early shaping of issues or debates?
- Are there any memorial areas or items in our church? What are they? Under what circumstances were they given and/or dedicated?
- What are the favorite stories and most unforgettable events of the early years?
- How was our church's name selected?

ACT II: The Golden Years
- What were the greatest growth periods of our church?
- Who were the pastors during those times and for how long?
- What were those pastors' themes, slogans, and mottoes?
- Who were the key lay leaders during the greatest growth periods? Who and what did they represent?

- What projects and new programs were initiated during these growth periods?
- What have been the issues and problems over which people have conflicted regularly in our church?
- When were buildings erected? What do these projects represent?
- Which events and persons from the era are "dramatic" and are still remembered and discussed and why?

ACT III: The Present Moment
- How does our church now reflect its beginnings? How is our church different from its founding dream?
- What is the prevailing feeling tone of our church: fellowship and love, guilt, fear, anger, service?
- Who received recognition in our church and for what?
- To what priorities does our church budget point?
- What forces keep our church as it is? What or who are the traditionalizing forces?
- What are the special celebrations of our church?
- If our church were one person, who would it be?

Are you now clearer about your church's founding dream? Was it a healthy kingdom dream? If an unhealthy dream, how will you help your congregation rewrite its script and develop a new life plan?

Churches, like persons, have three choices about their scripts: (1) We live our scripts, whether healthy or unhealthy. (2) We avoid our scripts, if they are unhealthy. (3) We transplant our scripts, changing them from unhealthy to healthy.

Replanting demands an awareness of the destructive pattern of the old script and a deliberate congregational choice to end the old and to commit to a new script reflecting a kingdom dream.

A new vision of the ministry your church can develop provides the surest route to a healthy ministry and a story worth telling.

Cultivating Redemptive Dream Stories

Stories shape dreams. As a boy, I read hero stories, mostly from sports and the American frontier. Little did I know, or care, that these stories were somewhat romanticized. I needed these models to imitate and dreams to live out. The same is true for churches. For that reason, Alex Haley's *Roots* saga became a national event, a folk event, and a part of our national history. As we discover ourselves, we find our own stories to tell.

Historical stories describe how we became the way we are. Our personal stories and folklore offer vehicles for understanding and transmitting our heritage. Putting life experience in story form makes abstract principles concrete and universal, as in Jesus' parables. These stories provide guiding clues to deeper realities.

Congregations brim with "clue stories." These stories tell what Dan McAdams calls "the truth in symbolic clothing."[8] They explain our churches to us. Clue stories function in several ways to inform leaders:

• Clue stories serve a **religious** function. They depict our sense of awe at the mystery of life. For example, Native Americans on the western plains thought the Great Spirit lived in the Black Hills. After seeing the beauty of those hills, I understand better why the Indians felt the Black Hills would be a suitable "home" for God. Furthermore, when the Hebrews wanted to tell of God's love and redeeming actions, they didn't philosophize. They remembered and retold the stories of Egypt and the Exodus. These events recounted their collective experiences with the God who had loved and redeemed them.

• Clue stories serve a **scientific** function. They give us pictures of our universe. For instance, during the 1906 San Francisco earthquake many residents of Chinatown tried to herd a bull back into its "place." These Chinese believed the universe was supported at its corners by four bulls. They reasoned that the bull they were driving had abandoned his post, destabilizing his corner of the world and causing the quake. Their panicked efforts further terrified the bull. A policeman finally shot and killed the raging bull. That action frightened the Chinese terribly. They no longer saw any hope of repairing their universe.

- Clue stories serve a **cultural** function. They support our social order and mold new generations. Art and history museums, ethnic festivals, and craft fairs overflow with explanations of how our society has developed.

- Clue stories serve a **psychological** function. They guide us through life's passages. Stories describe the emotional impact of adolescent rebellion, becoming a parent, and aging and retirement.

Clue stories grow up around the history of a congregation.[9] Dramatic events form the "campfire stories" of churches, describing key persons and happenings with shaping influence in a congregation's life, such as this one about a North Carolina country church:

The church was founded beside a bubbling spring. Community leaders claim the spring was discovered years ago when a slave woman and her children were dying of thirst during a drought. In despair of finding water, the slave woman prayed. Then, she found the spring. Since then, even during the longest droughts, this spring has never dried up. The community members interpret the spring as a sign of the presence and provision of God. Interestingly, this congregation has never had a major conflict involving the entire congregation during its 200 years of service. How is their story of God's constant care a factor in keeping their church healthy?

Kingdom dreams incorporate an epic quality. Participating in God's kingdom is a fact so comprehensive and a truth so majestic we constantly struggle to define and communicate it. This profound story provides the rocket fuel for the church's mission. The spirits and imaginations of Christians long for a story big enough and profound enough to tell and retell. In the face of gospel grandeur, our words and lives scramble to capture the power of God's ruling love fully.

Staying on Course

To have impact, a congregation's dream needs to be clearly known by its members. Yet, words rarely encompass kingdom dreams adequately. God's purpose of redemption exceeds our imaginations, hopes, and vocabularies. So, our continuing witness in word and life forms our best vehicle for telling his story.

Stating and publicizing your congregation's dream remains critical. Two stark options confront us as we tell our dream: Either the sharp focus of a congregation's life targets its dream, or the church drifts.

Drift begins early in congregational life. Oddly enough, early growth and success can dull the dream. Often, new members do not understand the seeds that germinated and made the congregation unique, so the focus dulls and drift begins. Even in the early stages of kingdom service, any congregation that attempts ministry without clear ties to its dream will drift. Goals generalize hopes, making it hard to stay sharply and publicly defined. The dulling of a sense of direction painfully challenges congregations.[10]

To resist these trends toward drifting from the dream, leaders will wisely take the following steps:

• Orient new members to and involve them in the congregation's dream.
• Be proactive and take initiative by weaving a plan with the leader's dream.
• Use all resources, including less-involved members, in the congregation's planning and ministry.
• Direct resources toward the needs of persons, not structures.

A fuller range of strategies to help your congregation shape its kingdom dream appears in chapter 10. For now, try to define the fundamental direction of your congregation through the clue questions in the following action exercises.

ACTION EXERCISE #3
The Stabilizing Taproot of Our Church

Basic Identity
• Who are we?
• What kind of ministry dream do we have?
• What kind of ministry dream "has" us?
• What's our level of organizational health?

Unique Contribution
• What is our unique contribution in and to our community?
• What is the special strength of our congregation?
• What is the distinctive nature of our ministry?

Primary Audience
• Who is our primary audience?
• Are our ministries, finances, and energies focused primarily toward our church family or beyond our church?
• How does our ministry tend to select particular age, social, economic, or educational groups?
• Which new audience(s) are we trying to reach?

Resource Use
• How do we use our basic resources: people, money, time, information, and physical facilities?
• Which resource do we value most? Least?

Strategic Game Plan
• How will we multiply our membership growth rate?
• How will we train our people for ministry?
• How will we leaven our community?
• How will we expand our stewardship potential?
• How will we enrich our own fellowship?

Our healthiest dreams focus on God's kingdom. If we narrow our dreams, however, we risk tunnel vision.

Curing Tunnel Vision

When Jesus taught his followers, he talked about the kingdom of God much more than the church—by a dramatic ratio of 40:1. Some congregations develop tunnel vision by majoring on their church, while minoring on the kingdom. These groups may ask too often, "How can we 'do church' here?" to the near exclusion of "How can we bring God's kingdom through this congregation?" A kingdom dream undergirds our methods with a theology big enough to cure tunnel vision.

Remember: Dreams seed and root congregational vitality. Leadership expert Robert Greenleaf notes: "Not much happens without a dream. And for something great to happen there must be a great dream. Behind every great achievement is a dreamer of great dreams. Much more than a dreamer is required to bring it to reality; but the dream must be there first."[11]

Make Christ's kingdom your dream for your church.

Notes

[1]Arthur Miller, *Death of a Salesman* (New York: Viking, 1958), 138.

[2]Daniel J. Levinson, et al., *The Seasons of a Man's Life* (New York: Alfred A. Knopf, 1978), 91.

[3]Gregory A. Boyd, *The Myth of a Christian Religion* (Grand Rapids: Zondervan, 2009), 78. Boyd prophetically challenges believers to put the kingdom of God above all secondary loyalties. His message stretches us, as the kingdom of God always does.

[4]William Herbert Carruth, "Dreamers of Dreams," in James D. Morrison, *Masterpieces of Religious Verse* (New York: Harper & Brothers, 1948), 278.

[5]Paul R. Lawrence and Jay W. Lorsch, *Developing Organizations* (Reading, MA: Addison-Wesley, 1969), 6 and 15.

[6]A. M. Hunter, *Interpreting the Parables* (Philadelphia: Westminste, 1960), 7. For additional perspectives on the parables as kingdom stories, see Joachim Jeremias, *The Parables of Jesus* (New York: Scribner's, 1955); A. M. Hunter, *The Parables Then and Now* (Philadelphia: Westminster Press, 1971); and Eugene S. Wehrli, *Exploring the Parables* (Boston: United Church Press, 1963).

[7]For treatments of personal scripts, see Claude M. Steiner, *Scripts People Live* (New York: Grove Press, 1974). To see how patterns move across generations, see the classic treatment by Murray Bowen, *Family Therapy in Clinical Practice* (New York: Aronson, 2002).

[8]Dan P. McAdams, *Stories We Live By: Personal Myths and the Making of the Self* (New York: William Morrow, 1993). For perspectives from Joseph Campbell, see "The Need for New Myths," *Time*, 17 January 1972, 50-51. For a helpful discussion of our need to experience again the power and imagination of the biblical record, see Guilford Dudley III, *The Recovery of Christian Myth* (Philadelphia: Westminster, 1967).

[9]For informative material on the defining power of organization stories, see: Stephen Denning, *The Secret Language of Leadership: How Leaders Inspire Action Through Narrative* (New York: John Wiley and Sons, 2007); Stephen Denning, *The Leader's Guide to Storytelling: Mastering the Art and Discipline of Business Narrative* (San Francisco: Jossey-Bass, 2005); Ian I. Mitroff and Ralph H. Kilmann, "Stories Managers Tell: A New Tool for Organizational Problem Solving," *Management Review*, July 1975, 18*ff*; and Leland P. Bradford and Jerry B. Harvey, Dealing with Dysfunctional Organization Myths" in Wyatt Warner Burke and Harvey A. Hornstein, *The Social Technology of Organization Development* (Fairfax, VA: Learning Resources, 1972), 244-254.

[10]Seymour L. Rosenberg, *Self-analysis of Your Organization* (New York: AMACOM, 1974), 28.

[11]Robert K. Greenleaf, *Servant Leadership* (New York: Paulist/Newman, 1977), 16.

Chapter 4

Beliefs: Anchors for Church Health

If kingdom dreams form the souls of our congregations, beliefs provide the pulsating hearts. Theology circulates oxygen-rich life blood throughout the body of Christ. How do you see your congregation's heart being filled and fired by beliefs?

Congregational beliefs, seeded by preaching, teaching, serving, sharing life, and singing, grow naturally. Rooted in theology, beliefs that launch and nurture kingdom dreams flow from sturdy theology. How do the worship, discipleship and fellowship approaches, social media, mission outreach, and music of your church reinforce or undercut your congregation's dreams? How do the beliefs of your church promote growth in faith and stand in contrast to culture?

As Bibles and hymnals lose more and more visibility, some worshipers wonder if sermons will survive to the end of the 21st century. Amid "worship wars" and debates about the merits of traditional, contemporary, and blended worship, our aim here is not to address worship styles, musical tastes, performance singing, or generational marketing. Rather, beliefs vibrant enough to undergird kingdom dreams capture our interest and nurture our faith.

Shane Claiborne challenges us to be sure faith makes a difference: "If the Christian church loses this generation, it will not be because we didn't entertain them, but because we didn't dare them. . . . It won't be because we'd made the gospel too hard, but because we made it too easy."[1]

God's kingdom, never a shortcut, reminds us that deep beliefs anchor church health.

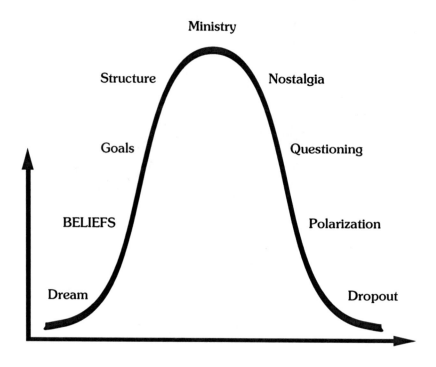

Wellsprings of Belief

In practice our beliefs flow from several sources. Fundamentally the Holy Book and the song book—words and music—shape our beliefs. The Bible records God's revelation of himself to us; the hymnal celebrates our response to God's love.[2]

In the Bible our salvation story sings its message. The birth of Christ inspired several hymns of praise: the Annunciation by Gabriel (Luke 1:30-33), Mary's Magnificat (Luke 1:46-55), the angels' song called *Gloria in Excelsis* (Luke 2:14), and *Nunc Dimittis* by Simeon (Luke 2:29-32).

Songs reach beyond the Gospels, of course. The first hymn in the Bible, Moses' song of victory after the Red Sea deliverance (Exod. 15:1-18), features praise for God's provision. Psalms, the Old Testament's song book, covers the full range of spiritual needs. Most scholars think the hymn sung by Jesus and the apostles after the Last Supper (Matt. 26:30) was a Hallel Psalm (Pss. 113118), also a song of praise.

The loftiest Christological statement in the New Testament (Phil. 2:5-11), appears to be a quotation from an existing Christian hymn. Persecution of the church produced the first Christian song service on record. Paul and Silas (Acts 16:25) set Jesus' words and works to music and sang "songs in the night."

The kingdom dream of Jesus and the Bible's theme of Christological praise link in Christ himself. Christ inaugurated the kingdom of God; the kingdom is completed in Christ. "Jesus *is* the Kingdom," according to one theologian.[3] Congregationally, God's kingdom dream anchors and enriches beliefs. As we mature personally, we grow beliefs sturdy enough for the demands of each succeeding life stage.

Belief Ladders

Imagine a "belief ladder" with higher and higher rungs. The belief ladder's lower rungs seed faith's beginnings for children and new believers. The middle rungs support young adults and growing believers as they discover belief's power. And, the higher rungs anchor mature adults and seasoned believers in the community's faith. Visualize beliefs growing stage-by-stage as higher and higher rungs on the ladder.

Get ready to climb belief ladders with three faith adventurers. And, for the moment, let's do something different and focus on music as a basic source of belief. Let's watch how beliefs develop from music over a lifespan.

New Believers

An eight-year-old brought her best friend to church with her. She gave her friend a quick orientation to her church's worship space. She pointed to the two books in the pew racks and said, "We have two Bibles here: the Holy Bible and the Singing Bible."

The little girl stated a profound truth. Although still a child, she knew intuitively that her own congregation was shaped by a variety of resources and practices. More importantly, she recognized the books that were already planting beliefs in her life. She was reading and singing her emerging beliefs.

Music speaks to children, who learn songs of faith at young ages and sing them throughout their lives. This little girl, already being shaped by the "Singing Bible," had found a key source for her growing beliefs. Her belief ladder invited her faith to begin with basics and to climb ever higher.

Growing Believers

A mid-range musical rung on the belief ladder gives words to the faith and emotions of young adults. Given words, beliefs spill over into our lives.

My college roommate was a committed Christian. But, like many church members, especially young adults, he didn't yet speak of his faith glibly.

One evening, while I was studying for an exam, another friend in the dormitory dropped by our room to chat. My roommate and the visitor somehow fell into a conversation about a hymnal. Before I realized what was happening, they opened a hymnal and began a loud and lusty duet. And, then they sang one song after another.

At first I was aggravated that they were being so noisy at a time when I needed to study. Then I became curious and finally fascinated by what was happening. They would leaf through the hymnal for a few pages, spy a familiar hymn, pounce on it like a priceless treasure, and "testify" about it. Usually they'd say something like, "Grandma loved this one! I remember her singing this song while she baked cookies." Then, they would raise the roof with the gusto of their singing. Whatever they lacked in harmony, they made up for in volume. Then they would return to the hymnal and repeat the scene again.

Several times during the hour they serenaded me, they cried over a hymn. They would recall warm, personal experiences related to the hymn, and say, "I love this song! Why don't we sing it more often at church?" The depth of their emotion in the singing and discussing of their favorite hymns caught me off guard.

I knew instinctively that this unusual display of religious fervor by two otherwise fun-loving college boys was very significant. They ordinarily would not (or could not) discuss their religious beliefs, but familiar hymns set free what they felt about Christ and his church. The doctrine they had absorbed from sermons, Bible studies, and youth groups overflowed into strong emotions as they sang.

Given words by hymn writers, these two university students expressed their Christianity that evening. The sound tracks in their heads played out loud and stirred their deepest feelings.

Seasoned Believers

Our personal theology, growing inside out, continues to flower over our entire lifetime. Although our beliefs may need some organization sometimes, we can tell our story of what God has done and is doing in our lives as we become mature adults. Let's climb to a higher, anchoring rung on the belief ladder with a first responder.

A North Carolina fire chief lamented about a church fire with an intensely personal dimension for him. He fought the fire that had burned down his own church. A personal and profound loss, the fire brought back deep memories: "Watching a church building burn where you have received so many personal blessings and remembering others who have also received so many blessings was a very hard thing to do. That's where I learned to sing my first song—'Blessed Assurance'—page 269."[4] He even remembered the hymn's page number in the congregation's hymnal!

When this fireman, now a mature believer, remembered his past faith experiences in that place and space, blessings from the community overflowed. His beliefs are stored high on the belief ladder to be used in making sense of life's experiences.

ACTION EXERCISE #4
Profiling the Beliefs We Sing

- Take a favorite hymn survey of the congregation.
- What hymns and songs do our congregation sing repeatedly and enthusiastically?
- What are the doctrinal themes and content of these best-loved hymns and songs?
- Who chooses the worship hymns and songs regularly? Does this selection role offer the possibility of special influence in shaping the congregation's beliefs? When the congregation-at-large chooses worship music, are there apparent differences in the selections? Is the doctrinal content different when the congregation selects the worship music?
- How do these favorite hymns and songs relate to, reflect on, or differ from the congregation's dream?
- How does our congregation's music anchor, celebrate, and extend its kingdom dream?

Our "belief ladders" of music give ways to grow in faith. Now, let's place our theology in historical and congregational contexts.

Tuning Theology

For those of us on the more emotional wing of the Christian family, church music provides a central theological resource. The music a congregation sings regularly and with conviction provides concrete clues to the congregation's collective theology. Some children who attend church regularly sing religious choruses before they can recite Bible verses. For the young and old, music shapes those who sing and hear it.

Congregations have traditionally relied on two key theologians: preacher-teachers who share faith in sermons and teaching sessions, and musician-teachers who choose the hymns and songs for worship and public gatherings. These leaders' theologies and musical selections combine into formative forces for the belief patterns of churches and their members.

Some church musicians advocate strongly for solid theology in today's worship resources. Kyle Matthews, a Christian songwriter/performer and Dove Award winner, left Nashville's music industry when he discovered that some writers of religious songs were unfamiliar with Scripture, thought mostly in terms of business, and thereby created disposable music for churches. Matthews challenges churches to adopt church music that undergirds theological education and Christian formation.[5]

Beliefs Growing Inside Out

Infectious faith: that's how C. S. Lewis described the contagious joy we find in Christ. There's a viral dimension to our beliefs, since our faith is more caught than taught. Our beliefs grow more organically than systematically and emerge inside out.

Experiential Faith

Personally, our faith stories grow out of our experiences. We ask, "What do I know about God? How is my life rooted in beliefs?" Experiential believers know their own journey, recognize the plots of holy ground in their experience, and tell their stories of God's activity in their lives.

Experienced theology, or how we believe, displays four unique characteristics:

1. Experienced theology emerges **intuitively and instinctually**. There's a sixth-sense quality about it, flowing through our pores without deliberate teaching and learning. It seems to know the lyrics and hum the music even without memorizing the score.

2. Experienced theology emerges **spontaneously**. It is contagious, free, emotional, and unrestrained, and its energy taps the internal wellsprings of natural enthusiasm.

3. Experienced theology emerges **repetitiously**. Habit, pattern, and recurrence mark a theology of experience. Actions and values based on experiential theology reproduce themselves repeatedly, almost automatically.

4. Experienced theology emerges as a **congregational expression**. Beliefs link persons within groups, knitting them together around their community's shared vision. Corporate life is bound together by a subtle sense of belonging that creates trust, identity, and communion.

We're not describing some random kind of folk theology here. The attitude of "Anything you decide to believe is fine. Just do your own thing" doesn't describe experienced theology. From our congregations' spiritual experience together, the body of Christ grows more aware of God's patterns in our faith pilgrimages. We look for, listen to, and share what we understand God is doing in us and around us.

Theology begins and ends with God and our experiences of him. God, who is personal, relational, and redemptive, stays active in all persons who are open to finding and following him. As believers, we experience God daily, both directly and around the edges of our lives. When we recognize and acknowledge the patterns of God's power in and around us, we theologize about our own expanding experiences, and we tell our personal stories of infectious faith.

Illuminated Faith

I remember where I was when my own beliefs took a quantum leap forward. In my sermon chair in my Kansas church study, I was reading something written by A. M. Hunter, a favorite theologian. He was preparing to talk about the core of Jesus' teachings. When I came to the bottom of the page, I remember thinking, "Whatever he mentions on the next page will be familiar to me. I've sat under strong pastors and good teachers. I've preached lots of sermons on Jesus' core teaching."

Then, on that new page, Hunter talked about the centrality of the kingdom of God. Like a dagger in my heart, I realized I'd never preached a sermon on God's kingdom. And, I'd heard precious little said about the kingdom of God in my former churches and classrooms. That moment froze me in my tracks.

How had I not read Scripture with larger lenses? What else had I missed? How many theological discoveries were ahead? How much more growth was coming my way?

I had a belief system with plenty of blind spots and biases. I didn't know what I didn't know. I didn't know how much more muddling awaited me.

After deep reflection, a theological light came on. I'd grown up in one of America's extremely individualistic and isolated regions. In that religious tradition we thought and believed one-to-one, soul-to-soul. So, my inherited belief patterns focused on individuals, not communities. My sermons featured the will of God rather than the kingdom of God. Unknowingly, I put a lid on my beliefs and blinded myself to some of God's richest lessons. How could I invite God's larger world to break into my life and ministry?

It took time for me to expand from thinking about God's will for individual believers to thinking about God's kingdom across entire congregations and cultures. Already a pastor, I was shocked by how small my perception of God had remained. A profound conversion, I began to discover heaven coming to earth in my congregation and far beyond.

Is your church limiting itself with blind spots or limiting beliefs? Place a spiritual stethoscope to your congregation's heart and listen with intuition. How familiar do the following comments sound?

- We have nothing to offer others.
- No one's interested in us.
- We're invisible.
- We're just not good enough to attract others.
- There must be something wrong with us.

Churches with big dreams about God's kingdom find healthier ways to live and minister. They move beyond their limiting beliefs.

Bridging Beliefs in Community

Although our core kingdom dream flows from Scripture, some of our beliefs about God may be more influenced by people and places than we realize. Our families, teachers, mentors, and ministers mold our beliefs and behaviors in piecemeal fashion. Additionally, our cultures and community backgrounds seep into our theology in ways mostly beyond our awareness.

One Heart, Many Veins

Our seminary-trained ministers may have studied theology formally, but most of our lay leaders discover their beliefs in the "seminary of bits and pieces." As we grow up and move from place to place, we absorb new and different faith streams. I once belonged to a church in Phoenix where three state groups and some stragglers had converged. We had a "Texas Club," an "Oklahoma Club," and an "Ohio Club." And, then there was a significant group of us in the "Other States' Club." We all gathered under the same roof and claimed the same denominational family. But, when we debated, we spoke different faith languages. We found that our varied backgrounds shaped our beliefs and behaviors more than we knew.

Geographic places and cultural backgrounds influence our beliefs. In the United States, we know Baton Rouge isn't the same as Boston. We've seen that the Rust Belt and the Sun Belt have different outlooks and atmospheres. We understand that Miami and Montana aren't cultural matches. We don't assume that Appalachia and the Pacific Northwest are similar regions. We've learned that Native Americans and immigrant Americans have heritages that vary from each other. We experience rural and urban areas differently. We absorb these differences from experience and observation. These differences in place and practice plant varying beliefs in us.

Common Conviction, Varied Stories

When Christians pool their experiences with God, a congregational body of belief emerges. Churches try to express their doctrinal stances formally through mission statements, covenants, confessions of faith, and even constitutions and bylaws. But these formal, written documents rarely reflect the group's living theology accurately.

How can we discover our congregation's belief system? How, then, can we move from varied personal stories to a common, congregation-wide belief system?

James McClendon helps us bridge from the narrative theology of our own stories to the connecting images of a convictional community such as a congregation. McClendon claims, "The best way to understand theology is to see it . . . as the investigation of the convictions of a convictional community."[6] What we believe and confirm, we affirm and do.

Our beliefs and theology appear most visibly when we act out our convictions in worship, witness, and ministry. Jesus gave us some visual celebrations to practice and many vivid stories to repeat. For example, the Lord's Supper celebrates theology-in-action, an event regularly enacted to remind us of Christ's death for us. Baptism gives a visual testimony to faith. Congregational beliefs grow out of our common history.[7] Congregations explore some key shapers of their beliefs and practices by examining their collective pasts.

ACTION EXERCISE #5

Shapers of Our Congregational Beliefs

- How has the profound faith of key leaders influenced us?
- What have been the most important decisions we have made as a group during our history?
- How do these decisions continue to shape how we believe and act?
- What are the special gifts of our congregation for which we're grateful?
- What hurts or conflicts do we still resent and need to face?

One Image, Multiple Expressions

Congregational leaders are typically more verbal than visual in preaching, teaching, and worship styles. Images from Scripture and hymns deepen a congregation's kingdom dream and become a primary resource for developing a healthy church. Interestingly, social media amplifies both verbal and visual impacts.

Verbal impacts. Verbally, ministers expand the theological imaginations of their congregations by the way they preach and teach. For example, two ministers on a church staff used a dramatic dialogue to explore the jailing of Paul and Silas (Acts 16). The sermon combined their testimony of why they risked prison for their faith. The congregation's hymn service began with the two ministers singing a duet and the congregation joining in on the "songs in the night." This made experiential theology a living reality and gave the congregation a heightened sense of involvement and participation.

On one occasion I led a youth group in a series of studies called "Now Sounds for New Christians." We selected several popular songs with strong messages, played and analyzed the themes of these songs, and then examined blocks of Scripture to see how the Bible dealt with these same issues. Most of the youngsters had never thought about how the music they constantly listened to was influencing them. Creating a conversation between music and faith helped them examine and mature in their values.

In a Lord's Supper service an electric moment emerged when during the retelling of the Last Supper story, four worshipers suddenly stood, one after the other on a prearranged cue, and asked, "Lord, is it I?" (Matt. 26:20-25). The impact was so profound, several worshipers reported they almost repeated the question aloud spontaneously. That's when experiential theology is really alive and well!

Visual impacts. Visually, a congregation's belief system also strengthens what's seen by congregants. After all, the eye has been called the window of the soul. But many churches make sparing use of visual theology. Visuals add impact to theological root systems.

A sculptor, a visual artist, joined his pastor in a sermon series on the Twelve Apostles. The two met each week to study the following Sunday's texts together. Then, before worship, the sculptor created a partial bust of that week's apostle. During the sermon the sculptor worked on one side of the platform, putting finishing touches on the bust. The busts were then fired and placed on permanent display in the church library. The sculptor, a long-time member of this church, observed, "I've never been asked to use my art at church."

A healthy belief system leads to the discovery of local expressions of a kingdom dream and to taking congregational ownership of that dream. Since worship is the most public occasion involving the largest number of members, the preaching, musical, and visual elements of worship strengthen congregational beliefs. Together, we observe the patterns of our faith pilgrimages, tell our stories, sing of the Christ who awakens our dream, and preach and teach to define our theology. Stewards of our beliefs and behaviors, we live the kingdom dream "out loud" and "in color."

Our opportunity is clear. We discover God's story, make it our personal and congregational story, and tell that story in word and deed.

A Change of Seasons

As you read ahead, you'll sense a change of psychological seasons. Chapter 3 described the kingdom dream of a healthy church. In chapter 4 we've explored a healthy theological foundation to support the dream. Both are more emotional and intuitive issues. In chapters 5 and 6 we'll explore goals and structures in healthy churches, usually more logical concerns.

It's an important transition. We'll be using different sides of our brains. Each of us tends to favor and use one hemisphere of our brain more comfortably than the opposite side. Some of us are right-brained, because we utilize primarily the right hemisphere of our brains; others of us are left-brained.

Let's compare and contrast the distinctive thinking styles of our two-brain hemispheres:[8]

- Those of us who rely mainly on the **right hemisphere** of our brain are more intuitive and visual. We think holistically and process multiple bits of information simultaneously. If we could peer into the right side of our brain, we would likely see things moving randomly in all directions, similar to the break on a billiard table. We right-brainers handle emotional ebbs-and-flows flexibly and think more "Eastern," as in the more interactive thought patterns of the Hebrews.

• Those of us who favor the **left hemisphere** of our brain think more rationally, more logically, and in linear fashion. We deal well with data, language, and sequences. If we could peek inside our left brain, we would probably see a column of soldiers marching crisply in orderly formation. This style of thinking is more "Western," as in the Greek thought patterns that dominate some of the New Testament and much of systematic theology.

Both brain hemispheres are needed for leading a congregation toward health. The diverse gifts in the body of Christ are especially crucial at this point (1 Cor. 12:14-26). The right-brained members of congregations can lead where the strengths of vision, imagination, intuition, and feeling are needed. Where logic, planning, and reasoning are demanded, the left-brained church members can provide their thinking-style gifts to organizational life.

It's interesting to note that the Bible tends to be more right-brained and holistic, while most formal theology is inclined to rely on the left hemisphere. American culture has also been shaped by the left-brain functioning of the Industrial Age.

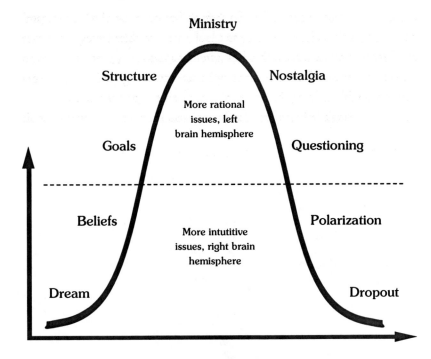

Your church is challenged to use its right-brain hemisphere to dream and then switch over to its left-brain hemisphere to develop and execute its plans. We believe God's kingdom calls for our whole-brain creativity and commitment. Balance in thought patterns is essential. This balance will stretch us, but it's necessary for church health and the use of spiritual gifts.

Get ready. We'll be using all our brain power as we dig deeper into church health.

Notes

[1]Krista Tippett, *Becoming Wise: An Inquiry into the Mystery and Art of Living* (New York: Penguin, 2017), 178-179.

[2]Edmond D. Keith, *Christian Hymnody* (Nashville: Convention Press, 1956), Also see David W. Music and Milburn Price, *Survey of Christian Hymnody*, 5th ed. (Carol Stream, IL: Hope Publishing, 2011).

[3]Harvey Cox, *The Secular City* (New York: Macmillan, 1965), 111.

[4]"That's Where I Learned to Sing My First Song," *Biblical Recorder*, 10 February 1979, 2. "Blessed Assurance" was ranked the ninth most popular traditional Christian hymn. See Renee Davis, "The Top 15 Traditional Christian Hymns," www.iBelieve.com.

[5]Jeff Brumley, "Songwriter Sees 'Good News' in Declining Role of Church Music," https://baptistnew.com/songwriter-sees-good-news-declining-role-church-music, 24 May 2017. Also see Tim Challies, 19 March 2017, https://www.challies.com/what-we-lost-when-we-lost-hymnals.

[6]James William McClendon Jr., *Biography as Theology: How Life Stories Can Remake Today's Theology* (Nashville: Abingdon, 1974), 35. McClendon suggests that we can understand a person's theology by understanding his biography. From outstanding Christians' writings, biographies, interview records, and reports from family and friends, McClendon extracts "controlling images or dominant motifs" of the persons he is studying. These images are acted out and form the "very substance of religion." See pp. 87-111 for an explanation by McClendon of his method of doing experiential theology.

[7]Sam Keen, *To a Dancing God* (New York: Harper & Row, 1970), 73. Keen, in the context of a discussion on "storytelling and the discovery of identity," lists four questions he uses to help persons explore how they've come to be as they are: What *wounds* or hurts do you resent having suffered? What *gifts* were you given for which you are grateful? Who were your important *heroes* and models? What were the crucial *decisions* for which you were responsible? I've restated these questions for a group or congregation to use in understanding what they believe and why they act as they do.

[8]For a technical treatment of brain hemispheres, see J. Graham Beaumont, *Introduction to Neuropsychology*, 2nd ed. (New York: Guilford, 2008), 134-156. For a sampling of classic research on brain hemisphere functioning, see Howard Gardner, *The Shattered Mind* (New York: Alfred A. Knopf, 1975); Michael S. Gazzaniga, *The Bisected Brain* (New York: Appleton-Century Crofts, 1970); and Henry Mintzberg, "Planning on the Left Side and Managing on the Right," *Harvard Business Review*, July-August 1976, 49-58.

Goals provide turning points for congregational action. Members make choices and take action. Turning points emerge. Given the determinative nature of goals, the futures of churches flow from their goals.

Mission and survival describe starkly the health-related watershed for congregational goal-setting. Classically, mission and survival contrast types of church goals. They define choices and directions in opposite fashion.[3] Either congregations join God in redemptive "co-mission," or they simply try to hang on.

Survival Goals

Survival keeps doors open, lights on, and organizational machinery turning. Survival tempts churches and other organizations to adopt a "safety first" attitude and simply build on what they have.

Ironically, the Pastoral Epistles to Timothy and Titus signal a subtle switch from missional action toward survival thinking. Just a generation or so into the Christian movement, these three letters already suggested a mood change from aggressive risk-taking toward a focus on safer, defense-oriented holding actions. Or, as Tom Long describes the situation: "In the Pastoral Epistles . . . we see the church on the mechanic's lift in the garage, and we are given guidance for performing an ecclesial engine overhaul."[4]

Written for those young in the faith, these three short letters hint at a shift from serving to pre-serving and con-serving. Notice how verbs of caution and resistance creep in: "guard" (1 Tim. 6:20, 2 Tim. 1:14), "avoid" (1 Tim. 6:20; 2 Tim. 2:16, 3:5; Titus 3:2), "shun" (2 Tim. 2:22), "have nothing to do with" (2 Tim. 2:23), "beware" (2 Tim. 3:15), "rebuke" (Titus 1:13), and "renounce" (Titus 2:12). Survival turns us toward an "anti" stance and away from a "pro" support of people and projects.

The Pastorals, though generally calling for steadfastness, do not demonstrate a blatant change of tone. But a survival mentality usually slides into the foreground quietly and without fanfare. The switch often begins with words. Listen to verbs, our language's muscle words, for signals that survival impels your congregation. Our language signals the seduction of a survival mentality taking over a church.

Goals and Stages

Mission and survival, pivot points in congregational vitality, define our goals. Interestingly, congregations at different life stages tend to choose different approaches as they develop survival goals.

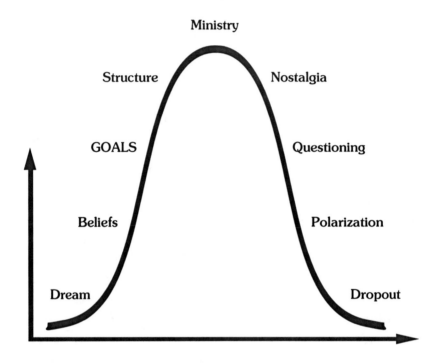

- **Emerging congregations** adopt those actions necessary for institutional life in early stages when congregations are most fragile. Their goals center on gathering a congregation, building a facility, and solidifying a budget. Think bodies, bricks, and bucks.

- Research finds that many **settled churches**, losing touch with their kingdom dream, or, worse yet, never finding a clear purpose at all, characteristically take one of two actions to survive: They conflict with and/or fire ministers as a vent for their frustrations. Or, they construct a building and plunge themselves into the clearer survival goal of paying a mortgage debt. Think blame or build.

• Many **plateaued churches** find survival goals becoming ends in themselves. Established churches drift into a problem-solving stance and find themselves constantly fighting brush fires. These stuck congregations give little or no thought to planning and being missional. Think driving with the transmission in park.

• Another challenge occurs when a **declining congregation** discovers that survival formed its founding dream. Even the early enthusiasm characteristic of a new congregation centered on survival tasks. Think living in a bunker.

Visualize mission goals on the upside of the health cycle and survival goals on the down side. Mission plans and looks to the future; survival solves problems and hangs on to the present.

Goal Shapers

A congregation's goals, formal or informal, flow from a variety of sources. Formal goals describe those actions the congregation explores and openly commits itself to do. Informal goals support relational needs in the congregation. Whether formal or informal, a congregation's goals divide themselves in either-or fashion around mission and ministry or around survival and maintenance.

Several key forces help shape the logic of congregational goals. Goal shapers bubble up from dreams and beliefs, from people and places, providing energy for congregational futures. Four of these goal shapers are especially significant.

Ministry Context

The "where" of settings and situations invites ministry. Increasingly, churches serve as spiritual anchors for their neighbors rather than simply providing housing for neighborhood activities.

As ministry settings change, so does goal setting. Toward the end of the 20th century, church long-range planning groups used time horizons of 7-10 years. Those groups did their work and then disbanded. In the early 21st century, long-range time horizons for churches are down to 3-5 years and shrinking. Churches see high-tech companies using 90-day goal targets with permanent planning teams to discern their futures.

The contextual shift in timeframes and perspectives is dramatic. The older planning method forecasted from the "present-forward." The emerging approach uses "future-back," looking ahead and then "backcasting" step-by-step from the ultimate goal to connect with the current situation. With churches focusing on their changing contexts more deliberately, planning is shifting to "outside-in" also. Without considering their internal and external intersections, churches end up missing both targets.

Leaders' Outlooks

According to William Rothschild, "Each leader . . . has a vision and strives to make reality conform with it. Some visions call for a complete transformation; others entail marginal change."[5] In churches the dreams of leaders—lay and clergy—spill over, mix with the hopes of the congregation, and emerge as goals.

Congregational Climate

An atmosphere settles over a church, tempering its outlook and, therefore, influencing its goals. Some congregations feel warm, optimistic, and proactive. Others feel apathetic and inert. Still other churches feel negative and defensive. The atmosphere or climate determines morale levels and sense of direction to a large extent.

Stakeholders' Expectations

Not all members of a church want a stake in organizational life, but some participants move from casual curiosity to deep commitment—potentially becoming the most powerful goal shapers. They develop and express a sense of psychological ownership. Stakeholders make an emotional investment of vision, energy, time, and money in their congregation. This psychological phenomenon parallels the stockholder who invests money in a publicly owned company.

Stakeholding goes far deeper than a mere sense of belonging to a group. For congregational stakeholders, the group's life belongs to them. Emotional ownership shows up in the formation and execution of congregational goals. Lyle Schaller defines a good goal as "one that I have had a part in formulating. A bad goal is one that someone else developed and wants me to implement."[6] Stakeholders take ownership of goals.

Stakeholders feel a personal involvement in, responsibility for, and loyalty to their church that goes beyond assigned or delegated tasks. Low levels of stakeholding in a church or volunteer organization show up in declining participation or financial support, low morale, staffing difficulties, communication gaps, and poor planning. Leaders multiply and link stakeholders, turning members into full-fledged partners.

When goals begin to draw congregations forward, the leadership focus changes from "what we will do" goals to "how we will take action" strategies. Goal strategies[7] grow out of the decisions of the goal shapers. These strategies range from proactive to remedial:

- *New expansions*, the most radical goal strategy, diversifies into totally new ministry areas and is willing to take risks to grow.
- *Extension growth*, a somewhat less aggressive strategy, builds on the congregation's healthiest DNA, selectively spinning off ministries from an already established base.
- *Preservation*, a common middle-of-the-road goal strategy, holds its ground and defends the ministries of the past.
- *Phasing out* occurs when ministries, past their peak, begin pruning away deadwood to reallocate precious resources.
- *Exiting* ministries is a remedial option for when the time arrives to cut losses.

Default Goals

Over time, organizations develop a life and momentum of their own. If unhealthy, they drift down the path of least resistance. Default goals dominate churches during times of drift. No one chooses or decides or directs. Habit and routine take over. Then, the organization uses its members' time, energy, money, and church properties without a sense of mission. Default goals show up in several varieties:

Repetition of the Past

Repeating last year takes the path of least resistance. Planning slides into a habit of doing again what has been done before. Leaders, then, struggle to maintain business as usual and to keep routines from becoming too deadening. Budgets and calendars get tweaked a bit, and the past is repeated one more time.

One minister, who had served the same congregation for a decade, summed up in graphic terms what life felt like when last year became the fallback position: "After having walked around this barn for 10 years, you learn where to step! We're totally predictable."

Ministry by repetition is ordinarily out of touch with the kingdom dream. Longer-term leaders, clergy or lay, are especially tempted to slide into doing the same things over and over.

Church Goals

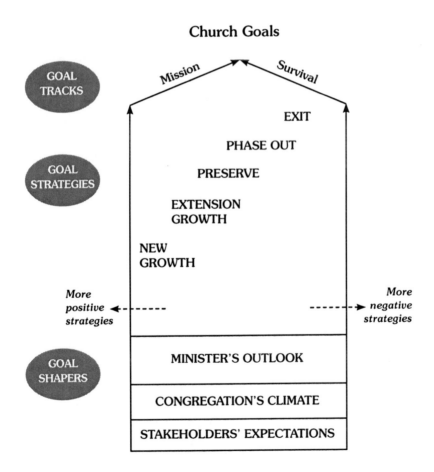

Real Estate Agenda

A real estate agenda can become a default goal too. Debt creates a clear-cut survival goal. With clear-cut legal and moral obligations, we pay off loans on buildings and properties. "Edifice complexes" and their debt loads drive some congregations.

One well-to-do young church made a crucial decision focused on mission or survival. It established itself successfully and paid off its initial building and property mortgages. With almost unlimited resources of people, finances, and talent, it looked at its missional options. Instead, the young church built an elaborate wedding chapel. Even though many of its members were influential citizens, they couldn't fill the large sanctuary with family and friends for a wedding. They constructed a smaller replica of the regular sanctuary and used it exclusively for weddings.

Plunging into debt makes real estate the survival agenda and limits ministry possibilities. Without clear ministry goals for the use of space and place, church buildings become maintenance operations—literally.

Busywork

Busy-ness creates a treadmill of activity to pass time, creating its own type of goal. Busywork sometimes shows that individual satisfaction has displaced group goals. When persons in an organization pursue their own goals and allow group goals to lag, the group settles for busyness rather than redirecting. Some tension between individual and group goals always exists in organizations, but the energy focus of healthy congregations remains on the redemptive dream of the larger body of Christ.

Kingdom dreams keep churches from settling into default positions. We look and move forward.

Goal Indicators and Owners

Church goals reflect personal and organizational values. We act on our values.[8] They provide the motivational catapults for what we achieve. A dream internalized and concretized by an individual becomes a personal value.

When congregations take ownership of the dream's values, those become the group's goals. Group values set the direction for organizations.

Our checkbook and calendar spotlight our personal values. How we spend our money and our time puts our goals on public display. Likewise, a church's budget and calendar display the living goals of a congregation. They also reveal a church's operating priorities and often develop a pattern of their own.

One pastor bemoaned the overcrowded calendar of his church. He feared, with tongue in cheek, that his congregation would have to cancel Christmas and Easter for lack of calendar time! He claimed that too many "traditional activities" threatened to crowd out high, holy days.

Budgets also get rutted so that old organizations and traditional projects get funded year after year—even if they no longer make an important contribution to the kingdom dream.

In a former church of mine the congregation chose to devote six months to intensive evangelism and outreach work. We agreed that funds and calendar time for all program organizations would be measured by their contribution to the evangelistic goal. The most difficult issue in pursuing this goal was the persistent "we've always done (or spent) it this way before" chorus. Even with the goal clearly defined and freely and overwhelmingly chosen, we discovered that personal and organizational ruts threatened to derail our congregational vision.

Goals and budget intertwine, but goals precede budgets. Goals, generally set first, lead to budget development. Otherwise, the budget emerges as the accidental goal system of the church. Either we fund our dreams, or we just dream of funds.

What do your church budget and calendar reflect about your church's dream? You may discover that they have lost their direct relation to the dream. If so, ministries or organizations no longer supporting the primary mission of your church receive disproportionate amounts of the budget and calendar time.

In addition to planning our expenditures of money and time to coincide with our goals, personal ownership of the goals plays an important role in their implementation. Unmet goals point to low commitment by stakeholders. But real goals, valued by stakeholders whether they are formal or informal goals, are usually achieved. People do what they feel strongly about.

ACTION EXERCISE #6

Values Shown by Our Budget

- On which of the following items does our church spend the majority of its budget?
    - buildings and properties
    - personnel and salaries
    - national and global mission projects
    - local ministry and outreach projects
    - church education programs
- Do our budget expenditures flow outward on mission or inward on maintaining our congregation?
- Which age groups are spotlighted via budgeted funds?
- Which organizations receive the most money?
- Do we have any organizations or groups that have no access to budgeted funds?

Christian organizations distinguish themselves, in part, with an allegiance higher than their organizational goals. Christian groups internalize their eternal, redemptive value system. Their dream transcends their short-term interests.

Leaders who want to create and implement real congregation-wide goals will involve as many people as practical in goal setting. Why? Because people support what they help create. When the formally adopted goals of a group match the individual values of group members, real goals become virtually irresistible.

Mission Goals

The "dreams becoming deeds" process appears often in Scripture and Christian tradition. Did you know that hospitals, orphanages, and hotels grew out of our Judeo-Christian influence and ministry? The Hebrew psyche never healed from the scars of Egypt's captivity. The Hebrews had learned what life was like when they had no voice and when no one had concern for their state and fate.

Consequently, the Old Testament often reminded the Hebrews to care for "the widow, orphan, and stranger at the gate." These abandoned spirits, at the mercy of life's situations with no protection, called out to people of faith. Over time, this ethical and religious concern incarnated itself in institutions of care. Hospitals, orphanages, and hotels emerged.

Leaders appreciate the reach and power of dreams and visualize their far-reaching possibilities for ministry. We continue to cultivate this rich legacy by supporting mission goals and by linking our goals with our dreams.

Supporting Mission Goals

When a congregation chooses to be missional rather than settling for survival, two supportive strategies are accessed.

First, leaders build on the energy reservoirs of the congregation. Leaders identify certain persons with energy for certain projects or issues. Their enthusiasm and excitement for their pet projects may be almost fanatical. Sometimes persons or groups in a congregation discover mutual interests, form a coalition, and pool their energies. When these high-energy reservoirs are channeled, merged energies supply significant resources for organizational life. Energy reservoirs show evidence of motivation. Scarce and carefully stewarded commodities, ministries bubble up from energy reservoirs.

ACTION EXERCISE #7

Looking for Energy Reservoirs

- What do people volunteer for in our church?
- What do our members show enthusiasm for, get excited about, and have a willingness to do?
- What does our church budget time and money for without hesitation?

Second, leaders channel recognition. Volunteers, paid in satisfaction, growth, and service, appreciate recognition. Without adequate recognition, even highly motivated volunteers lose their enthusiasm for work, and their morale erodes.

ACTION EXERCISE #8

Evaluating Our Recognition Pattern

- What are people honored for in our church?
- What does it take to receive a thank you, a public recognition, a certificate of appreciation, a memorial plaque, one's name listed in the worship bulletin or church newsletter, or a personal letter from the minister?
- Who is honored in our church?
- How are they honored, by whom, and when?
- Are some church offices partly or totally honorary, and how are these assigned?

Linking Goals with Dreams

The healthiest goals grow directly out of dreams and beliefs. People respond well to specific, tangible goals—goals with faces and futures attached. We all like SMART goals. To develop tangible mission goals, consider the following:

- Make projects and goals that implement the church's dream very "sense-able."
- Make goals so real and concrete that they can almost be seen, touched, and tasted.
- Use congregational resources, such as buildings and properties, as extensions of dreams.
- Make buildings a means to an end.
- Make facilities goal-driven.
- Use buildings as launching pads and ministry containers.
- Plan people-oriented ministry in and from buildings and properties.
- Use buildings to launch new ministries.
- Obtain professional planning assistance to help discover the longer-range needs of the congregation and community.

Always link your congregation's goals to its dream. That's the surest way to turn kingdom dreams into deeds of ministry.

Co-missioning for Dream Goals

Christians share in God's redemptive mission. We are on "co-mission" with him in turning dreams into deeds. Congregational leaders are always challenged to focus resources on redemptive goals. Several strategies can assist the development of dream goals:

- **Keep the dream public and visible.** Preach it. Teach it. Model it. Orient new members to it. Give members many opportunities to talk about God's work in our world. Help them experience redemption as "co-mission." Provide lots of opportunities to take the gospel outside the walls.

- **Formalize community-wide goals.** Arrange for forums where aspects of the dream can be examined, debated, clarified, and supported. New ideas from members will enrich and excite. Special interest groups may be confronted. The intent is to adopt formally stake-held dreams.

- **Establish priorities and targets.** No church is likely to accomplish its kingdom dream entirely through one budget or single calendar or lone ministry. Congregations are rarely that rich in resources. Slice off the most crucial and attainable aspect of the dream and go to work.

- **State goals specifically.** Goals, generalizations by nature, create targets. Translate your goals into concrete, limited, realistic, and important statements of action. Ministry projects lend themselves to finely honed goals. Remember: Workable goals are "SMART."

- **Distribute roles and responsibilities.** People support what they create. Stakeholder goals have built-in support and attract implementers. Broaden the base of participation so all may be involved in turning dreams into tangible deeds.

- **Evaluate at regular intervals.** When progress advances toward goals, celebrate. If a congregation veers off target, make a mid-course correction. Evaluation guides and refines congregational goals.

Turning dreams into deeds incarnates ministry. Just as God in Christ became flesh (John 1:14), today's Christians embody their dreams and turn them into incarnated deeds of ministry and mission.

Notes

[1]Clarence L. Jordan, *Cotton Patch Version of Hebrews and the General Epistles* (New York: Association Press, 1973). Jordan founded Koinonia Farms, helped launch Habitat for Humanity, and wrote the Cotton Patch version of sections of the New Testament. See *Cotton Patch Gospel* (Macon, GA: Smyth and Helwys, 2002).

[2]This variation of the SMART acronym is adapted from a class on work attitudes and job motivation at Pennsylvania State University, by Brian Francis Redmond and Nathan Janicek ("Goal Setting Theory Overview," psu.edu/display/PSYCH484, 2 October 2016). This article demonstrates how organizations apply classic and current goal-setting approaches.

[3]Donald L. Metz, *New Congregations* (Philadelphia: Westminster, 1967). Metz studied a small group of new Presbyterian congregations on the West Coast. His findings have a fairly wide application to churches in general.

[4]Thomas G. Long, *1 & 2 Timothy and Titus: A Theological Commentary on the Bible* (Philadelphia: Westminster John Knox, 2016), 1.

[5]William E. Rothschild, *Putting It All Together: A Guide to Strategic Thinking* (New York: AMACOM, 1976), 15.

[6]Richard Beckhard, *Organization Development: Strategies and Models* (Reading, MA: Addison-Wesley, 1969), 19; Rothschild, *Putting It All Together*, 20.

[7]Lyle E. Schaller, *Survival Tactics in the Parish* (Nashville: Abingdon, 1977), 161.

[8]For a classic explanation of values, see Louis Raths, Merrill Harmin, and Sidney B. Simon, *Values and Teaching* (Columbus, OH: Charles E. Merrill, 1966) and Brian Hall, *Value Clarification as a Learning Process* (New York: Paulist/Newman Press, 1972). For a view of values in institutional life, see Maury Smith, "Some Implications of Value Clarification for Organizational Development," *The 1973 Annual Handbook for Group Facilitators* (San Diego: University Associate, 1973), 203-211.

Chapter 6

Structure:
Muscle for Ministry

Our bodies need skeletons, sinews, and muscles to stand, lift, and move ahead. Our churches also need sturdy structures to reach our kingdom dreams. Healthy relational systems help organizations work well.

Most of us have a structural picture in our head of how the world works. After delivering a lecture on the solar system a century ago, an older lady confronted William James, America's first psychologist. She took exception to his explanation that the earth is a ball rotating around the sun.

Rather, she proposed to James, "We live on a crust of earth on the back of a giant turtle."

To avoid abrasiveness, James asked, "Madam, what does the turtle stand on?"

"You're very clever," replied the lady, "but I can answer your question. The first turtle stands on the back of a second, far larger turtle."

"But what does the second turtle stand on?" persisted James.

Triumphantly, the lady announced: "It's no use, Mr. James. It is turtles all the way down!"

Organization gives the kingdom dream something to stand on and ways to work. Structure provides stability, strength, and purposeful life.

Organization lends a muscular structure to churches. Formal organization exists to pursue ministry goals. Informal organization emerges to meet needs. Whether formal or informal, structure helps our congregations do their work "decently and in order" (1 Cor. 14:40).

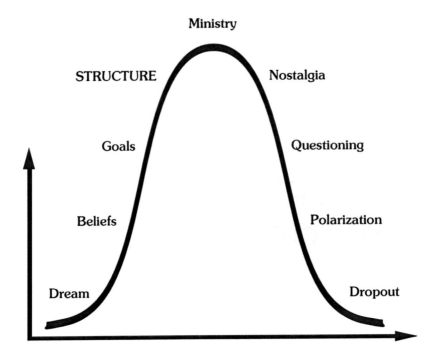

Formal Structure

Form follows function. This classic observation from architecture applies to organizational structure as well. Just as a dream yields beliefs and beliefs yield goals, an organization's formal goals point to the structure we select for pursuing our ministry goals. Structure organizes a congregation's dream, beliefs, and goals. Structure provides the flesh, bone, and muscle for our ministries.

Organizational Options

Several strong organizational design options are available to match a congregation's goals.[1] If your church and goals are traditional, your organizational structure selections may be pyramids and wheels.

• **Pyramids,** familiar in traditional organizations, focus authority and decision making in the hands of a few persons. There's a chain of command. Through multiple layers, communication flows down from the leaders to the followers in orderly fashion. Pyramids are efficient to manage, placing only a few men and women in top-level leadership. This type of structure is often used by denominations and churches with roots in the older Industrial Era.

- **Wheels** feature a central hub with spokes extending outward, as in the pods in airport terminals. Wheels centralize authority, decision making, and communication—much like pyramids. Teamwork and coordination are handled differently, however. Decentralized implementation of goals balances centralized planning. The wheel structure calls for cooperation across an organization's varied groups. Leaders of wheel-designed organizations must be strong coordinators, communicators, and managers of conflicting interests. The wheel model is used in denominations with widely scattered congregations. It's also now seen frequently in churches with satellite sites, drawing support and direction from an anchoring congregation or structure.

If a congregation and its goals are more complex and scattered, flexible and adaptive structures may be required. Newer, post-industrial organizational structures tend to be flatter, more flexible, and more broadly "distributed."[2] Most distinctively, distributed organizations use leader-follower partnerships. They show up as task forces, matrices, and networks.

- **Task forces** provide flexible design options for ad hoc or temporary groups. They set out to solve a single problem, pursue a single project, or produce one item. Special Forces in the military prefer this approach for its adaptability, self-reliance, and tailored missions. Some observers feel our society is increasingly gearing itself to what Alvin Toffler terms "ad-hocracy"[3] for non-routine goals and with disposable structures. Churches use task forces routinely. For example, pastor or staff search teams and special planning groups typically use task force structures. When their specific, assigned duty concludes, they dissolve and cease to function.

- **Matrices**, intersecting two functions at the same time, provide another design possibility.[4] In fact, project and matrix management form a separate, specialized field in management science. An outgrowth of America's space program, matrix organizations coordinate two functions, such as research and production, at once. The matrix approach requires so much specialized training and intense coordination that some volunteer organizations find it too demanding to manage comfortably. Some churches use a matrix structure if they're in transition or constructing new facilities, while continuing to manage ongoing ministries at the same time.

- **Networks**, emerging broadly, find models in the worlds of technology and media. Networks form associations of people who cluster around common callings or team up to pursue common interests. They move nimbly in as-needed fashion. Networks assist each other with information, support, and encouragement. We humans understand networks: we live daily within life-giving networks of nerves and arteries. Multisite congregations, too, are networked. Denominations and ministry organizations are now learning this structural language. Informally, our churches are peopled by human networks, similar to information grapevines, kinship circles, and organizational "power grids."

Form follows function. The ministry we provide or the goal we pursue points to the structure we use. Formal structure is important, because it either helps us reach our ministry goals, or it creates a systemic barrier that frustrates ministry and dulls the dream.

While organizational design options play a primary role in formal structure, relational and value systems are vital to the inner workings of the designs.

The Role of Relationships and Values

Organizations and churches are social systems with selected structural options to pursue their goals. Social systems are patterns of relationships with the following components:

- parts, or subsystems
- connections, or interfaces, making for interdependence among the parts
- synergy, or the whole being greater than the simple sum of the parts
- ripple effects when adjustments change the system and its subsystems and create the search for new stability

Think of your church as a social system. Churches have long sensed the organic nature of "the body of Christ" (Rom. 12:4-8, 1 Cor. 12:12-31). In a congregation the subsystems or parts are the relational networks, for example: classes, musical groups, fellowship clusters, and work groups. Connections or interfaces are seen in congregational councils and coordination teams where different subsystems meet and work. Synergy occurs when all or most of the membership own and implement the dream goals, thereby creating momentum and lifting morale. Ripple effects remind church leaders of a key systems' rule: You can't change just one thing. Any change jars the entire system and sets off a struggle for a new equilibrium.

A friend's experience with a brand-new car provides a homey illustration of how systems are interrelated. One Saturday morning he couldn't coax the transmission into gear. The shift lever moved freely but wouldn't engage. The car wouldn't budge. A quick examination by a mechanically-minded neighbor revealed a missing cotter pin in the shift lever, a tiny but crucial item. My friend complained to his wife about how shoddily cars are made these days and how all the enjoyment of having a new car was now tainted. She listened patiently to his description of a cotter pin and then handed him a paperclip. In a few minutes the clip became a temporary cotter pin, and the car ran like new again. One small item had shut down a large machine completely. A cotter pin seemed insignificant by itself but, in this case, was a vital part of the system. Interdependence is vital to systems.

Congregational leadership will do well to pay special attention to the relationship thread of social systems. People join churches to enter a system of relationships, both to Christ and to other members. If, over time, church members become relationally alienated from each other, they leave their church. Relational systems are the first exit, and, with the social connections broken, the larger church system becomes the distancing member's second exit.

Structure enables the pursuit of goals, but structure makes another important contribution. Structure embeds values, which calls for clear priorities.

One church prioritized its "form follows function" model precisely by structuring its priorities and placing people before programs, purpose over property, and kingdom community above kinship cliques. Like a guiding compass, these values brought the congregation back "home" time after time to the things that mattered most to them as a church.

Informal Structure

Martin Luther, thinking primarily of the church universal, described the existence of *ecclesiola* within the *ecclesia*—a "church within the church." One organizational expression of this subterranean phenomenon shows up in the informal organizational structure that develops within the formal structure of a local church.

Conflict occurs in organizations when informal needs do not match formal objectives. Not surprisingly, social ties and kinship loyalties, communication patterns, and organizational habits influence churches more than their stated goals. A church may vote to do a ministry and then ignore the implementation of that ministry, because that goal doesn't really match its personal interests.

Informal structure emerges spontaneously from the natural attempts of members to meet their mutual relational needs.[5]

Functional Needs

Informal organization serves functional needs in congregations such as knowledge, belonging, understanding, and protection.

We want to know. People in organizations need to be "in the know" and feel like insiders. Most organizations use formal channels for sharing information—social media links to websites, blogs, newsletters, announcements, and memos. But organizational participants are curious about more than official items. Therefore, organizations develop "grapevines."

Grapevines, intriguing and useful communication networks, deserve our ear for a variety of reasons:

• Information **originates anywhere** in an organization. For instance, the new president of a denominational agency quickly found that his best source of system-wide information was the organization's mailman. The mailman visited every work station twice daily and enjoyed such a wide range of relationships that he knew virtually everyone and everything. So, to take the pulse of the organization, the president learned to listen to the mailman. He also learned to cultivate the grapevine by telling the mailman selected tidbits that could be shared on his rounds.

- Information **spreads rapidly** in all directions. Like ripples on a pond, social media spreads information instantly with the click of a mouse.

- Roughly three of every four pieces of grapevine information **tend to be accurate**. However, inaccurate items usually are greatly distorted and can become examples of rumor mongering. But even rumors contain emotional messages that may be accurate: the content of the rumors may be untrue, but their feeling tone of fear or frustration may be on target.

- Grapevine information **can be coded**. Jargon and in-house jokes reveal meanings to insiders while outsiders are left uninformed or confused. The book of Revelation gives us a biblical example of this coded communication phenomenon.

- Grapevine information **selects its recipients**. Few people in an organization are on every grapevine. People can be deliberately bypassed and excluded from informal information networks.

- Sometimes **proximity affects the flow** of grapevine information. While leading a staff retreat for a huge church, I noticed the youth pastor was often addressed with "John, I don't know you, but . . ." After probing why John still wasn't known to his staff peers after three years of working with them, I learned that John's office was in the recreation building rather than in the church office area. The other staffers didn't know John because he was physically removed from them and was part of a different grapevine within a very large congregation.

I learned about community grapevines during my first student pastorate. When I would return to the church field at the end of the school week, I discovered the fastest way to catch up on community information was to call the local telephone operator. The rural area around my church was served by a central telephone switchboard with all calls placed by hand by an operator who evidently didn't hesitate to listen in. One call to her and the question, "Sarah, who are the folks who need a pastoral visit this weekend?" gave me information on the sick and struggling persons I needed to visit in my limited time on the field.

In a later pastorate I found that a network of women in the church spent long hours each day talking to each other on the phone. Whenever certain kinds of information needed to be circulated over the church grapevine, I'd call one of the "telephone ladies." An announcement such as "I know you'll be saddened to hear Mrs. Jones has just died. As you visit with people today, let them know about her funeral arrangements," never failed to get the word around the membership quickly on the informal grapevine.

We want to belong. People need close relationships. Each of us needs an occasional shoulder to cry on, a sympathetic ear for emotional support, and a hand with personal problem solving. Formal organizations target tasks and make relational issues secondary. So, when we need encouragers, sounding boards, and confidants, informal friendship networks naturally emerge to meet our need to belong. Why? Because formal goals rarely deal adequately with our need to belong.

We want to understand rules and expectations. Members need to be aware of the "rules" of their organization. The expectations and values of a group govern its behavior and attitudes. In some informal structures, for example, the expectations get translated into powerful mottoes such as, "You scratch my back and I'll scratch yours" or "Everyone pulls his weight" or "No one works too hard or looks too good." These statements of expectations are rarely formal policy, but members soon learn they are the rules and the ways to "belong" to a specific group.

We want to be protected. People know instinctively there's safety in numbers. Therefore, we band together to keep from being mistreated or oppressed. Collectively, people have power and courage to attempt things they wouldn't try individually. Lobbies, strikes, boycotts, and pressure groups supply prime examples of our tendency toward protection through group organization.

Because informal structure focuses on functional or psychological needs, it offers an untapped resource for ministers and other congregational leaders.

The Role of Leadership

Wise congregations use both their informal and formal structures well. The capacity to be good stewards of both structures—a tenuous balancing act—measures health in churches. Ministers and other leaders will do well to stay alert to at least three occasions when informal structure becomes especially crucial and runs counter to formal structures:

1. **When members feel that their personal needs are not being met:** Formal structure is geared to congregational goals more than personal needs. Rather than being threatened when natural needs for belonging, knowing, understanding expectations, and being protected surface, leaders can look for ways to minister through informal structures that develop automatically. Since informal structures meet needs, leaders ask questions:
   - What spiritual or emotional need isn't being met through formal channels?
   - Is the unmet need legitimate?
   - Could the need be met through formal structures?
   - If not, are we willing to use informal channels to meet real needs?

2. **When members question if leaders' care for them:** When the leaders of a congregation's formal structures listen to and show genuine concern for members, the informal structure becomes somewhat less important. The Golden Rule applies to organizations too.

3. **When members aren't involved in goal setting:** When church members have helped shape the formal goals of their congregation, the informal organization becomes less crucial. The deeper and broader the ownership of organizational goals, the more likely members are to trust the leaders and the formal structures.

If persons feel like outsiders to formal structures, they'll build informal systems where they feel like insiders. They'll create cliques if necessary. Wise leaders open up the formal processes of decision making and goal setting to all members. Then they use informal structures to minister humanely to persons who still feel marginalized.

For church leaders, formal structures pose management challenges. That is, resources must be focused on ministry goals. Management lends direction and order. Informal structures pose leadership challenges, however.

Creative leaders both manage formal goals and set the pace in meeting personal needs.[6] They help their churches develop goals that focus ministry in and beyond the congregation. And, they use informal networks to minister to members.

Every church develops a power structure, a pecking order of authority. If formal power structure and decision-making channels of a congregation close too tightly, an informal "underground" emerges to equalize or veto the power of the regular channels. When informal authority patterns run counter to the formal ones, it's usually impossible for formal authority to control the informal need for protection completely. In other words, closed power structures invite an "underground" to form for the protection of the less powerful members of the organization.

ACTION EXERCISE #9
Clues to Informal Structure

- If you wanted to test a ministry idea with someone in your congregation, with whom would you talk?
- Who is the key "legitimizer," the person who justifies ideas as fitting, reasonable, and correct in your congregation?
- Who is your church's "quarterback," the person whose power can reverse a developing decision or whose opinion can declare a ministry option out-of-bounds?
- When you have a personal burden, with whom do you talk about it in your church?
- If you had just returned from vacation and want to know what the church and community need situation is, whom would you ask?
- If you wanted to circulate ministry information, with whom would you share the information, and, thereby, cultivate the grapevine?

The Ministry of Organization

How much structure is enough for organizations? Just enough to carry out dream goals. Any under-organized congregation has aspects of its dream unrepresented by a focused organizational unit. An over-organized congregation either has organizational units that aren't vital to its dream or has units representing goals already met.[7]

While formal goals are rarely attained without organization, many organizational units outlive or outgrow their usefulness and call for pruning. Structure requires ongoing evaluation to keep it finely tuned for implementing dream goals.[8] Well-managed structure is the muscle and bone for pursuing dreams and goals in healthy fashion.

Ministers serve generalist roles within a congregation. From an organizational viewpoint, they are charged with seeing the big picture of the dream goals and maintaining a body-wide perspective.

Two types of personalities challenge ministers' system-wide view: (1) A "specialist"—someone who is a one-issue or a single-organizational unit loyalist—challenges the broader demands of leaders. Stretching this member's horizons allows him to take ownership of more of the congregation's dream. (2) A "generalist" challenges a body-wide vision. If leaders regulate their anxiety levels, the generalist member can become a valuable ally and sounding board.

Ministry through structure and throughout systems offers an exciting possibility for leaders who accept their stewardship of organizational resources. Structure and systems provide the flesh-and-bone strength and stability for pursuing congregational goals.

Notes

[1]O. Jeff Harris Jr., *Managing People at Work* (New York: Wiley & Sons, 1976), 79-108; Ross A. Webber, "Staying Organized," *Wharton Magazine,* Spring 1979, 16-23; Louis A. Allen, *Management and Organization* (New York: McGraw-Hill, 1958), 51-71; Ernest Dale, *Organization* (New York: AMACOM, 1967), 27-48; Joseph A. Letterer, *The Analysis of Organization* (New York: Wiley & Sons, 1967), 397-414; and Bertram M. Gross, *Organizations and Their Managing* (New York: Free Press, 1964), 197-237.

[2]William Bridges, "Leading the Distributed Organization," in Frances Hesselbein, Marshall Goldsmith, and Iain Somerville *Leading Beyond the Walls* (San Francisco: Jossey-Bass, 1994), 37-48. For a complete and technical overview of organizational structures, see Lee G. Bolman and Terrence E. Deal, *Reframing Organizations: Artistry, Choices, and Leadership* (San Francisco: Jossey-Bass, 1991), 79-99.

[3]Alvin Toffler, *Future Shock* (New York: Random House, 1970), 121.

[4]Stanley M. Davis and Paul R. Lawrence, *Matrix* (Reading, MA: Addison-Wesley, 1977); and Norman Wright, "Matrix Management: A Primer for the Administrative Manager," *Management Review*, April 1979, 58-61; May 1979, 59-62; June 1979, 57-58.

[5]Harris, *Managing People at Work*, 111-132; Keith Davis, "Togetherness: the Informal Variety," in Donald M. Bowman and Francis M. Fillerup, *Management: Organization and Planning* (New York: McGraw-Hill, 1963), 41-52; and Bertram M. Gross, *Organizations and Their Managing* (New York: Free Press, 1964), 238-259.

[6]Robert K. Greenleaf, *Servant Leadership* (New York: Paulist/Newman Press, 1977), 59-60.

[7]Arthur Merrihew Adams, *Effective Leadership for Today's Church* (Philadelphia: Westminster, 1978), 89.

[8]George S. Odiorne, "Clearing Corporate Deadwood: The Practical Art of Pruning Organization Limbs," *Management Review*, June 1979, 39-44; Ernest Dale, *Organization* (New York: AMACOM, 1967), 189-202; and Louis A. Allen, *Management and Organization* (New York: McGraw-Hill, 1958), 273-307.

Chapter 7

Ministry Dreams: Peaks and Valleys

Ministry, from the perspective of a congregation's intent, incarnates the kingdom dream "on earth as it is in heaven" (Matt. 6:20). The vision of Christian ministry comes to life in cups of cold water, visits to hospitals and prisons, and meals for the hungry (Matt. 25:34-40). Ministry offers words of witness to non-believers. It encourages the homeless, orphans, broken, aged, and marginalized. Ministry supports and heals persons with fragmented emotions and fractured relationships.

In short, congregational ministry extends Christ's redemptive outreach. Our ministry actions are limited only by our vision and the needs of others. Jesus plainly told and showed us what ministry looks like.

Ministry Peaks

In Luke 9 and 10, Jesus commissions his followers for ministry. The only Gentile writer in the Bible, Luke announces that salvation is for every person. Luke sees that Jesus lived and died for each of us—people from every corner of the world, from every language and culture, from every station, and at every stage. All of us belong to Christ, and, in Christ, there are no distinctions. The gospel is for everyone. Look at Luke's challenging instructions to ministry leaders and to congregations rooted in the kingdom dream.

Ministry Leaders

Kingdom leaders serve as **physicians** to souls and bodies. Luke reminds us that "Jesus called the 12 disciples together and gave them power and authority to drive out all demons and to cure diseases. Then he sent them out to proclaim the kingdom of God and to heal the sick" (9:1-2).

Doctor Luke, a medical practitioner himself, identifies three groups who need soul care: the demon-possessed, the diseased, and the sick. We help scattered and shattered souls root their lives deeply in God's kingdom.

Kingdom leaders serve as **missionaries** in a hostile world. Luke warns us: "The Lord commissioned 70 disciples and sent them ahead of him two by two into the countryside, saying . . . 'Be on your way. I am sending you like lambs into the midst of wolves . . . if you go into a town and find the people unfriendly, go into the streets and say, "This dust from your city that clings to our feet, we wipe it off in protest and to your shame." But understand this. It is still true that the kingdom of God has arrived'" (10:1, 3, 10-11).

Jesus didn't send out the 70 missionaries in pairs by accident. We need each other for mutual support and protection. Christ co-missions and partners us for ministry. We need faith friends when we go into an unfriendly world. Even amid hostility, God's kingdom continues to break in on us.

MINISTRY

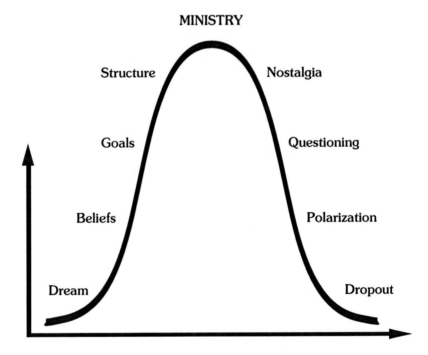

Structure   Nostalgia

Goals   Questioning

Beliefs   Polarization

Dream   Dropout

Kingdom leaders **partner in ministry** with other kingdom followers. Luke continues: "Travel simply as you go. Carry no purse or no bag for money or food. . . When you enter a home, begin by praying for a blessing on it. Stay there, eat what they eat, and enjoy the family's hospitality" (10:3a-4, 7).

When we find others who are faithfully saying "yes" to God, we join them. When we find those who are already living as citizens of God's kingdom, we say "yes" with them. Partners in ministry are precious.

Ministry Anchors

At the ministry stage on the health cycle, a church's anchoring kingdom dream enjoys fortification from its beliefs, goals, and structure. Ministry, the reason for discovery and discernment processes, stands empowered and ready—as in putting hands and feet into the calling of your heart. Spiritually and practically, ministry is poised for its future.

Several organizational characteristics identify anchors for a congregation at the ministry stage of the health cycle:

• **Ownership of the dream**—Members are on the same page emotionally and spiritually. They have enough stakeholders to sustain organizational life, and enough resources for inreach and outreach. Survival is now settled; mission and ministry are unfolding. Goals and structures are supporting the congregation's dream in practical ways.

• **Connected community**—Members know and trust each other, stand on a foundation of shared experiences and stable relationships, and work together in a friendly and connected atmosphere. They display a "we" type of congregational climate and are usually good neighbors and have found "third places" in the community, beyond the church buildings and members' homes, to meet and minister.

Groups versus the Group

Large groups generally cluster around smaller subgroups: "family groups," with longer-term, warmer, and more supportive relationships; "cousin groups," with some history of prior acquaintanceships; and "stranger groups," with relationships just beginning to bud. Smaller churches with effective ministries form primarily around family groups, creating surrogate or "second chance" families with intimate connections. Larger churches, usually a mixture of family and cousin groups with a smattering of strangers, explore new relational blends.

• **Ministry to human needs**—Formal goals and structure focus on concern for persons in and beyond the church. The informal organization ministers to the needs of members. Sam Keen observed about structured ministry: "Caring must be made concrete; otherwise there is no incarnation, no fleshing-out of love . . . Organization is the embodiment of love."[1]

• **Rewards to volunteers**—While spiritual and psychic rewards flow naturally, volunteers receive "pay" in the form of recognition, growth, and challenge. They feel blessed and extend blessings to others.

• **Increased morale**—The energy reservoirs of motivation are numerous, full, and available.

• **Healthy norms**—Organizational norms are growth-enhancing.

With some "peaks" identified, let's explore some organizational valleys.

Ministry Valleys

With God's blessing, the length and breadth of a congregation's ministry goes on and on, virtually endless. If ministry loses its focus on extending and expanding God's kingdom, however, an organizational plateau occurs. The congregation switches on autopilot, settling into a glide path. Ministry begins to slip, momentum ebbs, stagnation looms ahead, and organizational disease sets in.

Dimming of Dreams

The organizational aging process can be nudged along by, paradoxically, the congregation's strong commitment to practical ministries. Wise observer Lyle Schaller notes that "any move in the direction of becoming more sensitive to the needs of people increases the complexity of the operation."[2] A congregation either stays in touch with its dream and its unique opportunities for ministry, or the dream gap inadvertently shortens the duration of its effective ministry. Other factors can impede dream-based ministry too:

• Time passes and people forget basic purposes, beliefs, and beginnings.
• New ministers and new members bring varied backgrounds and interests.
• Congregational growth dilutes and subtly redefines the dream.
• Community needs and ministry opportunities change.
• No one deliberately refocuses on the dream, taking focus for granted.

Like barnacles collecting on the hull of a ship and slowing its progress, organizational aging bogs down ministry efforts. At first the slowing creeps along, almost imperceptibly. Later the sense of inertia and loss of movement becomes more obvious and frustrates leaders and members alike.

Almost inevitably, dreams dim for congregations. Churches can do many good activities for God and God's creatures, yet still lose the sense of being God's creatures and co-workers. Doing without being is deadening. Doing Christian ministry needs close and constant linkage to a kingdom dream to avoid losing direction.

Changing Directions

Leaders patrol organizational traffic circles, those crucial intersections where ideas meet, interact, and yield to help forward movement. In these moments both good things, such as cooperation, and bad things, such as bullying, happen. Intersections bring congregational life back to basics. "Why" monitors ministry traffic when values meet—and perhaps collide.

The ministry stage of church life refocuses the "why" of congregations, their calling and reason for being. "Why" powers and guides our ministries. Being called and committed to God's kingdom is our enduring "why."

Kingdom "crossing guards" stand watch when the "why" is magnified, ministry thrives, and the dream moves ahead. Staying on course with God's kingdom dream is basic leadership. Crossing guards also pay attention when an intersection shifts directions, usually slowly and subtly, the "why" blurs, and ministry wanders. Changing course when the dream is in jeopardy is an element of basic leadership.

Leaders understand how crucial the "why"—the acid test of the ministry stage—remains in church health. They watch for those intersections when the "why" changes direction—and then hold up a stop sign to avoid a ministry plateau.

Plateauing

Organizations die on autopilot. Coasting and admiring past victories lead to organizational inertia and health plateaus.[3] Since ministry plateaus stand the apex of the health cycle, the institutional situation appears secure, and that sense of security seduces us.

This quiet time in organizational life triggers lulls before storms. Soon some stakeholders grow uneasy with simply settling for the past and feel stuck. Then they will speak out and rock the boat.

Since the ministry stage is the dream's promise, organizational plateaus often arise after ministry successes or a period of growth. Several dynamics can work together to create this vulnerability:

• Leaders lose their personal touch as membership increases.
• Communication slows, and some members or groups miss needed information.
• Smugness follows a string of triumphs.
• The organization multiplies policies, procedures, and paperwork. "Paper-alysis" bogs down administrative processes in forms, reports, and requisitions, replacing person-to-person exchanges.[4]

Trying simply to hold the organization's position ignores storms brewing on the horizon, inviting decline. Several identifying signs of the organizational plateau appear:

• Inertia quietly sets in and begins to control.
• Tradition and history dominate.
• Experimentation and change wane.
• The leadership and power structure embed themselves.
• A clear pecking order emerges.
• Conformity and dependence increase in value.
• Ruts wear deeper and deeper.

- Growth slows, stops, and sometimes declines.
- Ministries struggle for leaders and participants.
- Giving levels and budget resources tighten.
- Budgets lose flexibility as debts or traditional expenditures squeeze new ministry options out.
- Member morale levels off, and energy reservoirs dry up.
- Available resources diminish, especially if leaders lose vision, the community changes, or the economy stagnates or reverses.
- Leaders stay in their comfort zones rather than move into their discomfort zones where new discoveries are made.
- The congregation substitutes "franchised faith" for the dream.
- Ministry overlooks contexts.
- Some churches follow their denomination's ministry proposals by rote instead of adapting suggested ministries and materials to their own unique dream and context.
- The organization's climate tilts subtly from healthy to unhealthy.

Not all of these occurrences happen in every church. Some plateau tilts take a while, while others happen quickly. Nonetheless, the ministry pace slows down and organizational illness deepens.

Just as physicians use diagnostic tools to name and select a course of treatment for physical illnesses, churches on the plateau need diagnosis and treatment too. Consider the following church plateau pathologies as coined by Peter Wagner:[5]

- "Ethnikitis"—the church isolating itself in a diverse community
- "Congregational geriatrics"—the church dying of old age
- "People-blindness"—the church ignoring cultural and sociological differences
- "Hyper-cooperativism"—the church choosing cooperative ministries to escape challenges that might create tension
- "Koinonitis"—the church focusing on fellowship and "serve-us"
- "Sociological strangulation"—the church bogging down in its own success from reaching one demographic or people group
- "Arrested development"—the church routinizing faith and ministry into tradition and social contact

These pathologies and others infect plateaued congregations. Recognizing both the plateau and the type of sickness provide diagnostic basic steps for congregations that are trying to get unstuck and begin ministering effectively again. While illness labels don't solve problems, they do provide a shorthand method of defining issues and a beginning point for discovering why the congregational dream lacks focus.

Underlying the "diseases" congregations "catch," a common health issue lurks: operating norms.

Congregational Norms

Norms reveal the habits of congregations or organizations.[6] Norms reflect the unconsidered "standard operating procedures" of a group. The unspoken rules, routines, and traditions of an organization give it unique identity. Norms are invisible understandings of "the way we do things here." In fact, norms explain the organization's "skeletons in the closet," those artifacts collected and stored away over the course of time.

Uncovering Norms

Leaders ask diagnostic questions for congregations in the ministry stage: How are the norms of our church healthy? How are our norms growth-encouraging or unhealthy and life-draining?

Norms provide a watershed for organizational life. If the norms reflect health and growth, ministry extends indefinitely. If, however, the norms embed illness and limit growth, ministry is stymied and invites decline.

Norms show a mysterious quality. They possess a strange power for conformity that's stronger than the influence of any single idea or lone person in the organization. A pastor, for example, preached a sermon with great passion. His eloquence and zeal caused his sermon to go on longer than usual. He preached right past 12 o'clock, the norm for the benediction in the congregation. Sensing a general restlessness among his listeners, the pastor angrily announced: "I don't care if every roast in Texas overcooks today! I'm going to finish my sermon."

The frustrated pastor finished his sermon, but he cooked his own goose in the process. After the service a child asked her mother, "What made the preacher so mad today?" The congregation soon forgot the content of the sermon—but they never forgot the breaching of their norms regarding time, anger, and courtesy. Although these norms weren't publically defined, the members expected something far different from their pastor. Clearly, a norm had been breached.

The pastor soon moved to a new church (and probably bought a new watch too). Hopefully, he also learned how brittle and explosive congregational norms remain. Like land mines, norms surprise and mutilate the unwary.

Time is one of the ripe areas for norms. For instance, we all have an idea of when a committee work session should end. If a concluding time isn't specified, a lot of group energy gets frittered away by members checking their watches (or cell phones) and fretting over the violation of their private deadlines. Time expectations and/or limitations are representative of many hidden or undefined norms present in a congregation.

Separating Norms from Standards

Norms and standards differ. Standards are what we say will happen; norms are what actually happens. Standards are customarily formal behaviors; norms are informal, but real, behaviors. Conflict flares when standards and norms become visibly and behaviorally dissimilar.

An interim pastor discovered the difference between norms and standards when he was moderating a business conference in a small Kentucky church in which the majority ruled in decision making. The little church's 20-30 members gathered for the conference in the sanctuary. After a hymn and a prayer the congregation settled down to conduct its business.

The interim pastor soon noticed a strange pattern. Even though the small congregation gathered on the left side of the center aisle, when a new issue came before the group for discussion, no one would speak at first and all eyes would glance immediately to the right. Soon it became apparent that the pianist and her husband, the only persons sitting on the right side of the church near the piano, drew the group's interest.

The interim pastor then remembered that the pianist's husband was the community's primary employer. Without words, he wielded so much power in the congregation that no other members stated their positions until Mr. Piano gave his opinion on the issue. Majority voting may have been the standard, but Mr. Piano's power was the obvious decision-making norm. Standards are ideals; norms are reality.

Working Toward New Norms

How then can norms be challenged and changed? Very carefully. And sometimes with great difficulty.

Like explosive mine fields, confronting congregational norms demands sensitivity, patience, timing, and skill. Walking through the mine fields of norms calls for a prophetic stance but a priestly mindset.

Some basic actions can help you explore your congregation's norms strategically:

• **Look for "tolerance zones."** Most organizations allow slight exceptions to their rules. Small margins of elasticity or deviation appear in emergency situations, in exceptional cases, or in the presence of celebrities.[7]

• **Identify current norms.** The early church believed that if a demon was named, it could be exorcised. The same principle holds with norms. Recognition precedes change.

• **Privately evaluate norms.** Are they health-inducing? Plumbing the depths of this question offers an early and stealthy step.

• **Take ownership of healthy norms.** Support, affirm, and use them.

• **Talk gently about norms.** Often the first public action, talking about norms must be done tenderly and within a stable pastoral or leadership relationship. Otherwise, confronting norms feels abrasive, and resistance becomes more entrenched and hostile.

• **Define new, healthier norms.** Jesus' story of the demon who returned with seven friends (Luke 11:24-26) and worsened the state of the once-free man reminds us of a principle of physics: nature abhors a vacuum. Organizations don't tolerate norm vacuums either. Unless constructive alternative norms are incorporated, an organization may be worse off than before the old norms were challenged. So, be patient, gentle, and strategic.

• **Practice new norms** as fresh behavioral rules.

• **Develop a standard first**. Norms, when aligned with standards, gather momentum from both the informal and formal systems of the organization.

• **Change healthier norms first**. Sick norms are apt to be more deeply entrenched in their pathology than norms that are simply marginal.

• **Attempt small changes** to ease norms' volatility. Building on healthy DNA generally offers an easier change approach than deconstructing a sick habit. The famed Bishop Pike regularly introduced radical change in his denomination by calling for a return to "tradition."

ACTION EXERCISE #10

Naming Our Organization's Norms

• What "rules" govern our church? Have these rules been violated? If so, how and by whom and at what cost?
• What do people feel free and easy doing in our church?
• What do people "have permission" to do in our church?
• What do people feel pressured to do in our church?
• What have people wanted to do but felt pressured not to do in our church?
• What have people felt pressured not to do and therefore avoid doing and feeling at ease?
• What issues trigger conflict?

Strategies for changing current norms and practicing new ones in congregations range from safe and relatively ineffective to risky but more effective.

Leaders can silently model new norms, a safe but less effective approach, or they can cause and manage ferment by talking about unhealthy norms publicly. More effectively, groups within the congregation may support each other gently while also confronting destructive norms. Most effectively but also most risky, congregations can take responsibility for examining and adjusting their own norms toward health.

Norms can empower ministry or block it. Examining norms can lead to changes needed for congregational health.

Decline or Change?

After the plateau phenomenon occurs in an organization, the climate shifts from healthy to unhealthy and decline begins. Early on, this tilt ordinarily remains unspectacular and unobserved. In a few cases the tilt is triggered by some dramatic or traumatic event. More often than not, the dream slowly erodes, and organizational decline slides into a pew, quietly blindsiding congregations.

Tilting Toward Change

Picture tilt as a contrast of a regenerative organization with a degenerative one.[8] When some critical characteristics appear on continua from high to low, the contrast becomes clearer.

REGENERATIVE ORGANIZATIONS		DEGENERATIVE ORGANIZATIONS
Hi ◀-------------------- Trust ----------------------▶ Lo		
Hi ◀------------------- Openness ---------------------▶ Lo		
Hi ◀----------------- Stakeholding -------------------▶ Lo		
Lo ◀-------------- Experimentation Risk ---------------▶ Hi		

While the use of the terms "regenerative" and "degenerative" refer to organizational concerns in this context, some theological implications emerge too. Regenerative systems are dream-based and oriented toward planning. These organizations have momentum and can't lose for winning. Degenerative systems are doubt-based and oriented toward problem solving. They are bogged down in the mire of inertia and can't win for losing.

Observing initiative is a quick way to determine if a congregation is a regenerative or degenerative organization. How is initiative used? Does the organization spend its energy planning or problem solving? Is time used proactively or reactively?

Another method of dramatizing the tilt from a regenerative to a degenerative organizational climate contrasts unhealthy congregations and healthy ones, as in the lists below:[9]

UNHEALTHY CONGREGATIONS:

- Any dream is narrowly owned by an elite few.
- Decision making is a top-level function only.
- During crises, members withdraw and blame each other.
- Territory is defended.
- Leaders feel isolated and act alone.
- Members compete.
- Personal needs are less important than organizational goals or vice versa.
- Conflict is seen as sinful, destructive, and to be avoided.
- Innovation is surrendered to tradition.
- Open discussion and disagreement are discouraged.

HEALTHY CONGREGATIONS:

- The dream is owned by a broad base of members.
- Group participation in decision making is common practice.
- Crises challenge and unify members.
- Leaders invite suggestions, feedback, and critique.
- A team atmosphere and shared responsibility are apparent.
- Members cooperate.
- Formal goals and personal needs are both treated as important.
- Conflict is viewed as inevitable, constructive, and to be used for personal and organizational growth.
- Innovation and experimentation are low risk and encouraged.
- Agreement and disagreement are both acceptable, and unhealthy agreement is confronted.[11]

Healthy congregations move toward hope, are more able to meet challenges and adapt to changes, and minister with and to their members instead of around them. Healthy congregations know who they are and where they are going, and respect the gifts and personal callings of various types of leaders.

Seeking Balanced Leadership

Every Christian carries leadership responsibilities. As persons grasped by Jesus' dream of the kingdom of God, Christians are responsible for implementing the dream, for doing ministry. Leadership becomes one application of the Reformation principle of the priesthood of every believer.

In my observation, churches are populated by several types of leaders. Each type of church member has a distinctive slant on the congregation's dream and has, therefore, a slightly different sense of responsibility for the dream. The question is: Who will become a multiplier for the kingdom dream and for congregational health?

- A **quarterback**, the congregation's most powerful signal caller, determines directions and goals to a significant extent. Power for the quarterback results in congregational service, resources, or community influence.

- **Legitimizers** are in the middle of decision making. They exercise influence either to bless or block ministries by their support or opposition. Legitimizers often form an informal inner circle for leaders and become sounding boards for ideas.

- **Lobbyists** form special interest groups within congregations. Lobbyists are usually one-issue members with a favorite doctrine or program they support to the virtual exclusion of all others. Some lobbyists would probably prefer to be legitimizers, but they aren't in the inner circle for some reason.

- **Founders**, cousins of lobbyists, are often long-term members of the congregation. If not charter members, they at least feel and act as if they began the enterprise. In younger churches, founders may be the visionaries of the congregation and lobby for the dream. In older congregations, founders become traditionalists who reflexively lobby for the past amid change.

- **Negatives** are folks who are against everything as a matter of style and principle. They have learned that being negative is often more powerful than being positive. However, many negatives don't have the flexibility to pick and choose their issues. They tend to be uniformly opposed to all new approaches.

- **Church neurotics** are sometimes negative, but generally confused. They either know of a problem in the congregation or cause one. After crying "wolf" a few times, only negatives and newcomers pay much attention to neurotics.

- **Activists** serve as backbones of congregations. They attend worship, teach classes, give time and money, visit prospects and shut-ins, sing in musical groups, chaperone youth groups, and live out their dream daily. Activists pray and participate, work and witness, lead and follow.

- **Wise members** are the spiritual giants of the congregations. Their judgment, counsel, and spiritual maturity provide the most precious resources of any congregation. They are the ones others turn to quickly and naturally for advice; they are ministers to all.

Balanced leadership undergirds church health. Whether pastors and staff or laypersons, some leaders are conceptualizers and others are operators.[11] That is, some leaders have the gift of dreaming, while others have the gift of doing. For a congregation to be healthy, transforming leadership needs to be present in strength and balance.[12] Balance in ministry includes both prayer and action, membership growth and social ministry, evangelism and discipleship, reflective study and assertive involvement.

Healthy congregations do not depend solely on pastors or leader teams for their kingdom dream. Although a church's minister is a pivotal person as the congregation's most public leader, the entire congregation is responsible for church management. All the members help direct church resources toward church goals. The pastor, staff, and leader corps guide the day-by-day implementation of church-wide goals and try to maintain an overall perspective of the congregation's dream and ministry.

From Here to Eternity

Ministry is what a congregation does daily because of its vision of God's kingdom. Ministry should be endless and ageless as it is empowered by the spirit of Christ. Too often, however, as churches grow, they either become more complex or they age and become tradition-bound. Then,

.ational decline sets in. Fortunately, decline in organizations can be
.d or at least minimized.

Unfortunately, not every congregation is ready to dream again. Laodicea, one of the seven churches of Revelation, had a devastating distinction. It was the only church of the seven with nothing for Christ to affirm (3:14-22). The condition of the church was tragic—paralyzed and doing nothing about its stuck state. Neither hot nor cold, Laodicea's church was fit only to be vomited up by the Risen Christ.

Ministry is killed by indifference. Is that warning enough for congregations that are tilting toward inaction and disease?

Notes

[1]Sam Keen, *To a Dancing God* (New York: Harper & Row, 1970), 109.

[2]Lyle E. Schaller, *The Pastor and the People* (Nashville: Abingdon, 1973), 106.

[3]R. D. Baker, Truman Brown Jr., Robert D. Dale, *Reviving the Plateaued Church* (New York: Convention Press, 1991); George S. Ordiorne, *How Managers Make Things Happen* (Englewood Cliffs, NJ: Prentice-Hall., 1961), 7-17; Lyle E. Schaller, *Hey, That's Our Church* (Nashville: Abingdon, 1975), 39-50.

[4]Lee Grossman, "A Manager's Approach to the Paperwork Explosion," *Management Review*, September 1978, 57-61.

[5]C. Peter Wagner, *Your Church Can Be Healthy* (Nashville: Abingdon, 1979).

[6]Eliza L. DesPortes, *Congregations in Change* (New York: Seabury, 1973), 199; Edgar H. Schein, *Process Consultation* (Reading, MA: Addison-Wesley, 1969), 59-61.

[7]Jurgen Ruesch, *Knowledge in Action* (New York: Aronson, 1975), 200-203.

[8]Adapted from Robert T. Golembiewski, *Renewing Organizations* (Itasca, IL: F. E. Peacock, 1972), 30-32.

[9]Adapted from material by Jack K. Fordyce and Raymond Weil, *Managing WITH People* (Reading, MA: Addison-Wesley, 1971), 11-14.

[10]William G. Dyer, *Team Building* (Reading, MA: Addison-Wesley, 1977), 93 ff.

[11]Robert K. Greenleaf, *Servant Leadership* (New York: Paulist/Newman Press, 1977), 66-69, 96.

[12]James MacGregor Burns, *Leadership* (New York: Harper & Row, 1978).

PART 3

Unhealthy
Congregations

Chapter 8

Nostalgia: Remembering Better Days

We don't often see a "Condemned by Order of the City" sign nailed to the front door of a church, but I saw that ominous sign on the big double doors of an Old First Church in the Southwest. Beside the condemned sanctuary stood a new, temporary metal building housing a worship center and church offices.

For years the congregation knew the sanctuary's balcony had pulled away from the walls. The congregation discussed the building's condition periodically over several years, but reached no decision. Finally, the city government declared the building unsafe for public use. Even then the congregation avoided the dilemma of either renovating or removing the old sanctuary.

I couldn't imagine what had brought Old First to such an impasse. When I asked a long-time member to explain the situation, he said sadly: "We couldn't bring ourselves to change a thing in the old building. After all, it's where Dr. Big Name preached back when he was our pastor in the 1930s and 1940s." The memory of former days under the ministry of a well-known pastor paralyzed the Old First congregation. That's nostalgia.

After a congregation reaches a plateau and the organizational balance tips toward degeneration, nostalgia flowers. Nostalgia, in an organizational setting, introduces the attitude, "It isn't working as well as it used to, is it?"

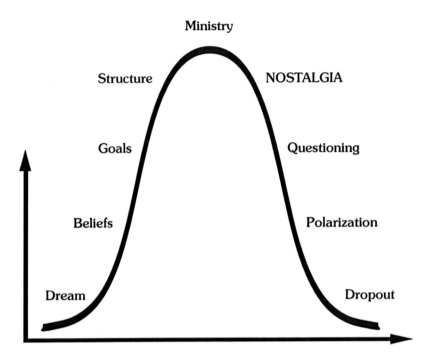

Nostalgia reflects an exile mentality.[1] Fulfillment hinges on the "once upon a time" remembrances of yesterday. "I remember when" stories become commonplace. The golden days are remembered fondly. From an organizational perspective, nostalgia signals the beginning of a wistful love for the past, eroding relationships, putting trust on hold, and a loosening commitment to present ministries and challenges.

Nostalgia, popular now in religion, politics, and culture, spurs conversations about returning to greatness and lobbying for simpler days. Nostalgia conventions provide a place for Americans to display or sell old record collections, political campaign buttons, and antique cars. Simpler yesterdays are preferred to uncertain tomorrows.

The word nostalgia derives from two Greek works, *nostos* (to return home) and *algia* (a painful condition). Homesickness is our equivalent English word. The term was initially applied to Swiss mercenary soldiers who became despondent and melancholy while fighting in foreign lands. These soldiers became homesick for the Alps and for calmer periods of their lives.[2] Change or unpleasant circumstances trigger wistful longing for past memories in all of us.

Homesickness appears in congregations too. The early stages of organizational decline manifest nostalgia. Flowing from change, nostalgia afflicts mobile societies and organizations in transition. Nostalgia is experienced by persons "who do not like where they have arrived and have no taste for the next destination."[3]

In organizational settings, nostalgia is that feeling of being caught between eras. The future threatens, the present is uncertain enough to cause tentativeness, and only the past seems safe and attractive. Congregations get mired down between their glory days and future shock. Nostalgia frustrates organizational leaders.

Nostalgia focuses congregational attention internally. An insider's mentality tries to preserve what has been and forfeits much of its ability to adapt to new demands. The struggle to survive saps congregational energy.

The Varied Faces of Nostalgia

Nostalgia faces three directions: past, present, and future. Each represents a slightly different feeling in persons and their institutions.

Past

Nostalgia longs for a return to "the good old days." As a result, contemporary America earns the descriptor of a "retread culture."[4] Re-creations, spin-offs, sequels, and remakes are the rage of our popular media. Nostalgia idealizes Mayberry.

Nostalgia suffers from selective memory. As Charles Kuralt, the late CBS television commentator, observed, "There are three kinds of memories: good, bad, and convenient." From a distance our memories magnify the pleasant and shrink the unpleasant. We romanticize triumphs and blot out tragedies. The blunt bottom line, as Gerald Clarke expressed it, is this: "Nostalgia selects only what is agreeable, and even that it distorts or turns into a myth."[5] We want to retreat to greatness without defining when we thought we were greatest. In the wise words of Will Rogers, "Things ain't what they used to be and probably never was."

I grew up amid an example of nostalgia's selective memory. My parents matured during the Great Depression of the 1930s, a desperate era, but I remember my grandparents and others speaking warmly of how families banded together and how close to God people became during the depression. Their wistful tones implied that if another depression came, families would stabilize and religion would revive. My grandfather often announced, "What this country needs is another good depression!"

To check out the realities of the Great Depression, I reviewed several hours of old theater newsreels from the '30s. The poverty and desperation of the era were stark, with soup lines and suicides common. But the "camp-fire stories" told years later gave a much more generous slant.

We humans edit bad times from our memories. So, we nostalgically recall the 1930s with little of the economic hardships, the 1940s with only war heroes, the 1950s without the witch-hunts of McCarthyism, the 1960s without Vietnam, the 1970s without Watergate, and the remainder of the 20th century without a Cold War.

Nostalgia hungers for the way we were. But the "good old days" probably weren't really ever that pleasant—except through the filters of romanticized memories.

Successes can seduce a congregation into only looking back toward the past. Businessman and author Herbert Prochnow counseled: "Forget the past. No one becomes successful in the past." That sentiment is half-true. We can learn from the past, but we can't live in it again.

Present

Nostalgia weakens our commitment to the present. This sentiment threatens declining organizations. Nostalgia's preference for the past leaves little energy for today.

It's always tempting to give primary allegiance to our familiar pasts. Some people tend to be more objective, however. For example, while struggling with terminal cancer, the late political optimist Hubert H. Humphrey evaluated yesterday's good old days in a televised interview: "They were never that good, believe me. The good new days are today, and better days are coming tomorrow. Our greatest songs are still unsung."

In nostalgic moments it's tough to remember that yesterday is dead and to realize that tomorrow is blind. When we select one or the other, we abandon the one not chosen.

Nostalgic congregations fall into "if only" syndromes and consider turning back to better times instead of renewing their dream and forging new ministry initiatives. This phenomenon is a threat and challenge to the kingdom dream and to organizational planning. Unless energy can be found for the present, the future dream of a congregation may become a nightmare.

Future

Nostalgia provides a fragile bridge to the future. More positively, some continuity between past and future is provided by nostalgia.

Upheaval triggers nostalgic periods of history. Think about the past century of American history: the Great Depression, World War II and the atomic bomb, the Korean Conflict and the Cold War, the Vietnam War, political assassinations, the Watergate scandal, inflation and recession cycles, and the "9-11" bombing of the Twin Towers and the Pentagon.

It's easy to see why we wish for easier options, a slower pace, and a happier era for our lives. Emotionally, we want to repeat some good old days. Nostalgia lends a sense of psychological stability, an oasis in history. Nostalgia gives us a toehold amid turbulence. A retreat into a "safe" past may remind us of our roots and free us for a foray into the future. Nostalgia is proof of our past, and the past can be our stepping stone into tomorrow.

While in the World War II death camp of Auschwitz, psychiatrist Victor Frankl experienced the past-present-future link that nostalgia provides. Amid the cold, sickness, emotional desolation, and spiritual poverty of the Holocaust, Frankl thought back:

> In my mind I took bus rides, unlocked the front door of my apartment, answered my telephone, switched on the electric lights. Our thoughts often centered on such details, and these memories could move one to tears. Then, one night a fellow prisoner passed the word of a spectacular sunset to the tired and hungry inmates. Everyone quickly went outside and silently absorbed the colors and shapes of the clouds. Finally, a prisoner broke the silence, "How beautiful the world *could* be!"[6]

Such experiences provide continuity in our lives and the courage to go forward.

Celebrating the past can, on occasion, provide historical continuity for tiptoeing into the future. For this reason, temporary retreats into the past in events such as homecoming and special recognitions of long-time leaders can help bridge the past-present-future link we face constantly in a rapidly changing world.

For example, a Lutheran church on the booming urban fringe of a large Texas city suddenly found itself changing from a quiet, rural congregation into a dynamic, growing suburban church. It outgrew its small, traditional building. A building committee, after study, recommended a modernistic architectural style for its new building. The committee found two mindsets, traditional and progressive, about equally represented in this changing congregation. As a result, the architects designed a small chapel-prayer room, a miniature of the old sanctuary, into the new structure. Long-time members found this familiar spot a nostalgic retreat as many other facets of the church's ministry changed rapidly around them. Interestingly, new members also sensed stability in the space. A sense of physical continuity helped this congregation both celebrate its past and journey into its future.

The Demands of a Nostalgic Church

Sliding into nostalgia provides early warning signals to leaders. Let's explore some examples.

Dealing with Corporate Depression

Change can be upsetting to congregations. What depression is to an individual, nostalgia can be for an organization. Just as loss or anger triggers depression in some people, we may become angry when our institutions grow so complex that they seem unmanageable. Then, since we can't confront a huge organization very directly, our anger turns inward, and we beat ourselves down emotionally. Or, we might feel a loss of control over our lives when bureaucratic problems become so large and tangled that we can't unravel them. Again, our futility turns within and we become depressed. In fact, the level of morale can sink, and the emotional tone of an entire organization can dampen and become depressed.

The poet Alfred Lord Tennyson noted, "Tears rise in the heart . . . thinking of the days that are no more." Congregations also need to grieve on occasion. But since grief is especially difficult to express in group settings, congregations feel corporate depression and express it as nostalgia.[7] The past is glorified, and there's little energy for the present.

I once observed a stark example of organizational depression in a church where I was a member. Our pastor resigned after several years of successful ministry. A couple of weeks after the pastor left, an important leader election was held. The election was a fiasco. First, members weren't even motivated to vote. Second, the vote was so scattered that no clear consensus developed. Third, many persons, even though they led in the vote totals, refused when they were asked to serve. Finally, those who agreed to serve had little enthusiasm for their future tasks.

Taken together, these reactions helped the congregation realize we were grieving and depressed. Members subsequently gathered to share our concerns and receive some "group therapy." We agreed to set the election aside, face our grief until it was resolved, and then resume our ministries. In retrospect, the congregation made a mature decision. Soon the depression ran its course. After we had expressed our grief, ministry efforts began again in healthy fashion.

How can a congregation deal with corporate depression? Using the example cited above as a case study, three guidelines appear.

1. Depression is generally cyclical. After we recognized we were mired in corporate depression, **we realized the depression would pass in time** with a bit of attention.

2. **We vented our pent-up feelings** of confusion, frustration, and anger over "abandonment" by the former pastor. Our church leaders met and explored the situation first. Then we staged a forum in which we openly discussed congregational grief and depression. Our interim pastor also preached a sermon on coping with the loss of a group's primary public leader. (If social media had been available then, that interactive channel might have reached some members on the periphery and ministered to their grief as well.)

3. Just as therapists often recommend exercise for their depressed clients, our congregation moved forward. **We began actively planning for our future** journey toward its kingdom dream.

The underlying dynamic in conquering corporate depression is raising a congregation's self-image and its confidence level. Therapists describe
this action as raising the relational "stroke economy" of an organization.[8]
Nostalgia can help the process of stroking and building confidence by
deliberately reviewing past successes as a springboard for new ventures in
ministry.

Discovering New Meanings

Ministers and other leaders help their congregations discover new meanings. While the gospel message doesn't change, we are constantly forced
to make new applications of it. Christianity is always only one generation
away from extinction. If we ever fail to meet new challenges for ministry
during a single generation, the church will become a religious dinosaur.

Visualize two streets intersecting at your church. One street carries its
traditions: biblical, theological, denominational, cultural, and geographical.
Traditions are the ways we've done ministry in the past. We get nostalgic
over our traditions.

The second street carries your church's contemporary challenges:
changing lifestyles, shifting family patterns, chemical dependence and
abuse, unreached people groups and new generations, an increased interest in leisure, an aging national population, and emerging technologies.
These issues present opportunities for congregations to evangelize, teach,
and interpret the gospel to unchurched lives.

These two streets symbolically meet at the church. Rather than an
intersection that invites a head-on collision or stop-and-go traffic, think
of the meeting of these streets as a traffic circle. At roundabouts the traffic
continues to move, with each of us yielding the right-of-way to others as
is timely and appropriate. This traffic circle guides our applications of our
kingdom dream to contemporary life situations.

Jesus depicted the process of making new meanings for a group in the
Sermon on the Mount. Repeatedly, he spoke of the truths stated "by them of
old" and then confronted them with new ministry applications in his "but I
say unto you" challenges. Discovering new ministry meanings from the base
of the old message is a creative leadership opportunity for every generation
of leaders. Finding and expressing these new meanings is an alternative to
lounging in nostalgia—and a challenge to congregational leaders.

ACTION EXERCISE #11
Measuring Our Church's Nostalgia Quotient

- Of how many different events, persons, or concerns can I imagine members of our congregation saying, "I remember when . . .?"
- What ministries, programs, or practices would our congregation be talking about if the members said, "It isn't working as well as it used to, is it?"
- Which eras of our congregation's history are remembered warmly and often?

Ministering in a Nostalgic Church

Corporate nostalgia makes unique demands on leaders. Several guidelines are helpful in facing the nostalgic congregation creatively:

- **Nostalgic members provide an early warning of systemic decline.** The presence of persistent and widespread nostalgia through a congregation is a signal that decline has begun and revitalization measures must be applied immediately.

- **Nostalgic members are usually friendly toward leaders.** Their wistfulness and longing for the past grow out of their traditionalism. They are the conservators of old victories, but they can remind leaders that organizational slippage is in process.

- **Leaders are often threatened by nostalgia.** When the inevitable allusions to the past are made during nostalgic periods, mature leaders protect themselves emotionally against comparisons that feel unfavorable. After all, nostalgia is an organizational phenomenon, not an individual attack.

    In a former church of mine a fire had occurred during a congregational growth boom. While the burned building was under construction, the church worshiped in a tent. One Easter more than 900 people gathered under the tent for worship. Although 10 years had passed since that all-time high attendance record had been set, members would speak longingly of the fire, the tent, and the "900" worshiping in the tent. Since fewer people attended the church during my era, I often felt threatened by references to the fire and its aftermath. (In my twisted fantasies I sometimes wondered what it would be like to set another fire, rent a tent, and return to the glory days!)

- **Nostalgia is an emotionally cool phase of organizational life.** The longing and the wistful sentiments are not angry yet. Leaders need to act to revitalize a nostalgic institution before cool emotions heat up.

- **Nostalgia, in strictly organizational terms, is a doubting of structure.** The temptation is to restructure, often a cosmetic strategy for organizational renewal. Restructuring may yield a brief surge of energy and favorable response, but complete remediation requires examination and reshaping of organizational goals The structure that nostalgia remembers so fondly may no longer represent the current goals of the church.

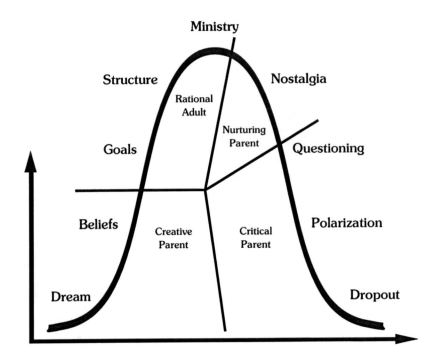

A major task of the leader of a nostalgic organization is to keep conversations flowing between traditions and contemporary issues. Nostalgia, to some degree, always represents the tension between who we are now and where we have been earlier. Momentum for new ministry grows out of shared meanings as members find new ways to apply the gospel to life.

Lull Before the Storm

The nostalgia phase of organizational life provides a lull before the storm. Steeper decline and escalating conflict are likely to follow. Therefore, the relative quiet of nostalgia offers an early warning signal of the need for an initiative toward congregational health.

Nostalgia overwhelmed the Old Testament exiles. The Psalmist lamented their demoralization and described their state of being frozen in inaction: "By the waters of Babylon, there we sat down and wept, when we remembered Zion. On the willow there we hung up our lyres. For there our captors required of us songs . . . How shall we sing the Lord's song in a foreign land?" (Ps. 137:1-4).

Wise leaders will take seriously the early warning signs of nostalgia in congregations.

Notes

[1] Sam Keen, *To a Dancing God* (New York: Harper & Row, 1970), 7-8.

[2] Fred Davis, *Yearning for Yesterday: a Sociology of Nostalgia* (New York: Free Press, 1979), 1.

[3] "Past Shock," *New York Times Magazine*, 4 May 1975, 6.

[4] "The Retread Culture," *New York Times Magazine*, 26 October 1975, 38.

[5] Gerald Clarke, "The Meaning of Nostalgia," *Time*, 3 May 1971, 77.

[6] Victor E. Frankl, *Man's Search for Meaning* (New York: Washington Square Press, 1963), 61-63.

[7] A case of national depression in political concerns is documented by Alexander and Margarete Mitscherlich in *The Inability to Mourn: Principles of Collective Behavior* (New York: Grove Press, 1975).

[8] Claude M. Steiner, *Scripts People Live* (New York: Grove Press, 1974), 323-334.

Chapter 9

Decline: Descending into Organizational Hell[1]

Lowell Thomas, the legendary broadcaster and journalist, overreacted to a news story when he was a cub reporter. In his autobiography, *Good Evening Everybody*, Thomas tells of returning home to Cripple Creek, Colorado, as a brand-new college graduate and taking a newspaper job. When a town fire occurred, he used a bold typeface usually reserved for posters and handbills and ran the headline, "Blaze Sweeps Local Buildings!"

An old newspaperman observed what Lowell Thomas was about to do and asked, "Exactly how many buildings burned?"

"Three," replied Thomas a bit sheepishly.

"I'll tell you what, kid," drawled the seasoned journalist. "I'd try to hold something back for the Second Coming!"

Evidences of hastening decline in our churches touches off our organizational "catastrophe reflex." Declining congregations glimpse disaster looming on the horizon. Questioning, polarization, conflict, and apathy point to three dynamics: worse and worse, faster and faster, and angrier and angrier.

Congregational climate decays rapidly during the descent into conflict and organizational illness. When decline begins, churches show more self-absorption with less interest in self-examination. Health wanes, and wellness fades from the radar.

A full-fledged congregational health check-up is necessary. Without a complete health assessment, we turn inward and turn on each other. That speeds the loss of vitality, magnifies tensions, and puts us on a downward rollercoaster toward danger.

The Fright of Church Fights

Many church leaders and church members freeze when conflict bubbles up. We welcome competition in athletics and tolerate cutthroat tactics in the marketplace, but we're scared of conflict in the church. It's time for us to understand why we do not like congregational conflict and, when it occurs, to learn to respond appropriately and not overreact. Christians do not like congregational conflict for several reasons:

- **We expect churches to be communities of reconciliation and wholeness.** Although conflict is a natural phenomenon that can be handled constructively, we fear that conflict will divide and weaken our congregation's witness and image in the community.

- **Some people feel conflict is less than Christian.** We may expect all Christians to believe the same doctrines at the same level of commitment and act on our convictions by supporting the same ministries, but to feel that Christians never disagree overlooks the rich differences between persons and groups.

- **We may never have experienced the power of the negative.** Edgar Schein observed that in working groups it takes three positive statements to offset one negative statement.[2] In other words, a negative response is three times more emotionally powerful and disruptive than an affirming word.

As a leadership coach, too often I had seen an angry outburst or a speech of opposition freeze a group's ability to act. I decided to test Schein's observation for myself. During a role-play session in a leader training lab, I waited silently until our mock church staff reached a decision, and then I verbally attacked the minister playing the pastor's role. My verbal assault had two results: the decision was reversed, and the pastor never spoke again during the role play.

Being against something can be a heady stance. "Anti" attitudes are on regular display in religion and politics. Now I understand one reason why some people oppose whatever is happening in their congregations. "It'll never fly, Wilbur" is generally heard with more impact than "Amen, sister."

Whether we like conflict or not, it's here to stay—even in the church. Conflict remains a spiritual concern. As congregations decline, their vulnerability to conflict in its various forms and stages increases. The tensions may begin with questioning, then move to polarization, and finally to disengagement by some members.

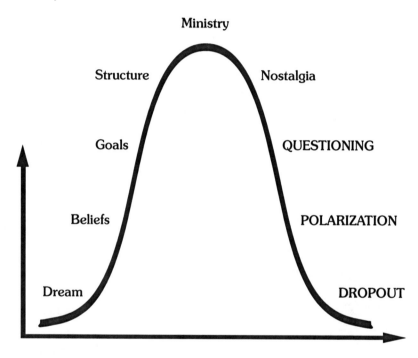

Questioning

If the early warning value of nostalgia is ignored, the organization soon moves deeper into decline. Serious questioning begins. The tone of the inquiries changes to doubt, irritability, and anger. The goals of the organization come under fire. Questioning raises important issues:

• Is this the right goal for our church?
• Are we on the right track?
• Should our church provide this ministry?

Casual responses or the denominational party line answers are no longer adequate. Glib responses will not satisfy serious questioners.

Without direct and effective organizational revitalization measures, the crisis lies dead ahead. The point of no return has been reached. Either the conflict will be resolved or at least managed at the questioning level, or it will destroy the organization. Questioning is the "now or never" point of congregational health. Health or death are the choices.

Signs of questioning appear in the behavior of members. An executive of a declining company described the organizational "death watch" process he observed as his business died:

> When a complex organization begins to fall apart, it doesn't go all at once: it isn't like a bomb in the cellar or a plane crash. It happens in bits and pieces, a fissure here, a missing part there.
>
> The process starts with the people. They become angry. Or frightened. Or restless. They take longer lunches. They change their work habits; those who worked long hours now work less; those who took it easy begin to show up on time and leave later. They talk a lot about the man at the top.[3]

The same process happens in churches. The questioning stage of congregational life indicates deepening organizational disease. Questioning, the "emergency room" stage for congregational life and ministry, turns on the alarm clock.

If questioning is the last chance for renewal of earthly congregations by human effort, though, thankfully it's not God's last word.

God's redemption has sturdy foundations. The kingdom of God is always coming, always bringing heaven to earth. God redeems us every day—past, present, and future. Believers affirm: "I have been redeemed. I am being redeemed. I will be redeemed." We and our churches are always works in progress.

God transforms communities we have put in a spiritual death spiral. We are saved by hope (Rom. 8:24-25), as well as by grace and faith. We may give up on each other, but God isn't through with us yet. He awakens hope and renews kingdom dreams, drawing us back from the brink of death and destruction. God only waits for us to invite his redemption.

At the questioning stage, the ball is in our court, but the clock is running out. Either we invite God's healing and renewal, or we die.

Polarization

With an inadequate response to questioning, doubt intensifies and polarization deepens. Now, basic beliefs are doubted. Faith in this congregation's future is waning fast.

While a great deal of congregational conflict is triggered by personality clashes in their varied guises, battle lines can also be drawn along doctrinal, political, or ethical lines. The "Is this right?" questions of the previous stage are now answered with strongly emotional reactions. Some members respond with conviction: "No! That isn't right. It's wrong. We can't 'do church' like that any longer." Other members are just as vigorous in answering, "Yes! We must continue to 'do church' like that." Sides and issues have been chosen, and lines have been drawn in the sand.

Conflict is now open, escalating, and messy. "We" *versus* "they," "this" as opposed to "that," and "right" or "wrong" issues define the congregation. As polarization wedges congregational factions apart, churches divide or at least become immobilized, both within and beyond their membership.

Our views about conflict shape the ways we deal with congregational polarization. Our assumptions regarding conflict determine our coping approaches:[4]

- **Conflict indicates a basic relationship.** It takes enormous energy to disagree or fight with others. When we engage in conflict with other persons in our church, we generally have a fairly strong relationship with them. Their positions matter. In other words, church fights are rarely between strangers. Conflict shows enough caring to expend the energy and time necessary for dealing with our differences.

- **Close relationships create more threatening conflict.** There's more at stake in conflict when both friendships and issues are involved. Additionally, good friends and intimates know where their opponent's weaknesses and sore spots are. Plus, the sense of being betrayed by a friend escalates basic disagreement into red-hot fury.

This dynamic causes many church fights to degenerate into personality clashes. The primary "facts" in personality-based conflict are feelings, the negative feelings of foes. Issueless conflicts, or "fights over nothing," ramp up the heat, because the energy focus is the way we feel about the other, our enemy. Fights among friends invite dirty tactics and leave lots of debris.

• **Higher investment and ownership mean keener conflict.** Stakeholders are generally the principals in organizational conflict. Church conflict becomes especially volatile because it deals with religion, a core value, along with emotional concerns of members. When people feel strongly about an issue, conflict tends to be sharper and more destructive.

Sometimes fringe members are also drawn into church fights. Even if they haven't been deeply involved in the congregation's life immediately before polarization occurs, the conflict offers them an opportunity to "buy in." Re-entry of fringe members into the mainstream of congregational conflict doesn't always indicate an interest in the specific issue of the conflict. A church conflict may serve as a catalyst for old disagreements and offer a new "cause" for general opposition. Unfortunately, conflict has a magnetic quality.

• **Group conflict introduces even deeper disagreement.** Individuals have arguments, but groups start wars. Groups idealize their positions and make all issues black-and-white polarities. Whereas an individual may recognize that her motives are mixed, groups diffuse motives and encourage a righteous attitude toward their stance. Blinded, "they" become the enemy.

In war, foes typically choose nicknames or terms that dehumanize their opponents. Then, horrible vengeance can be taken against our foes with little guilt or remorse. Why? Because foes are seen as less than human. Or, in church conflicts, opponents get names that imply a lesser faith.

• **Healthy congregations have more frequent, but smaller, conflicts.** Mature congregations recognize that differences enrich them. But when the "lid is kept on," pressure builds up and major decisions become battlegrounds. Polarization often occurs when a major conflict is brewing, and members have suppressed conflict in the past. They, therefore, have little experience in dealing with conflict. And, the church may lack a trusting forum where different views are explored openly. Stable congregations deal with their differences as they occur. They release pressure before it rises to dangerous levels.

- **Suppressing conflicts leads to dangerous conflict.** When a congregation suppresses conflicts, it stores up grievances. Finally, the sack of conflicts bursts and overflows, followed by a major explosion. As mentioned before, conflict involves enormous energy. When that energy is bottled up rather than managed, pressure builds to dangerous levels. Healthy congregations stay up-to-date on their conflicts and manage them well. Small conflicts, easier to resolve, remain less threatening to the congregation's dream.

Polarization creates an unhealthy atmosphere in a congregation. It indicates that conflict hasn't been dealt with early or resolved constructively. As polarization deepens, the gulf between persons and groups widens. Even if people elect to remain in the same congregation with people on the other side, energies may be used primarily to resist each other. When polarization occurs, ministry loses momentum and the congregation slides into disease.

Dropout

Apathy results from an organization remaining unresponsive to the nostalgia and differences of members. In the face of a "who cares?" congregational climate, some members give up and drop out. No longer do they have the energy to struggle for change, or else they become completely disillusioned by the depth of hostility demonstrated amid polarization.

As a result, they feel nothing deeply either pro or con about the congregation. They "sell off" their stake in the church. Their alienation toward the organization is total, and, perhaps, final. For them the kingdom dream has died in this church setting.

A study of the 80,000,000 unchurched Americans by Russell Hale describes eight major categories of persons outside organized religion.[5] One group is made up of "burned-out" persons or church dropouts. Although persons in this group were once heavily involved in congregational life, they wore down and exited. For one reason or another they felt depleted and decided against such an intense level of church participation. Unhealthy congregations load too much responsibility on too few persons. They quickly become candidates for religious and organizational burnout.

My observation? Only about one church in ten makes any concerted effort to recover its dropout members. As one church leader announced about members who had left his church, "They can just get glad the same way they got mad!" In other words, no current member intended to reach out to the dropouts. Their exits felt like rejection to those members who were left behind.

Several reasons explain a church's apparent disinterest in dropouts. Church leaders assume that dropouts are hostile. But, hostility isn't inevitable. Quite likely, if it was ever a factor, their anger is spent. In fact, their lack of feeling for their church may indicate a complete loss of emotional loyalty. Some leaders miss the vast reservoir of potential ministry by volunteers resting dormant on the fringes of their church. The peripheries of congregations may be home for wounded members from earlier conflicts. Many human resources are being wasted when experienced leaders retreat into mere observer roles.

When members drop out of their church, their dream for that faith community has died. Hope is gone for them in that place.

Sensors on the Fringe

While some church members leave their church in a period of conflict, some committed members simply move to the fringes of the congregation. They are half in and half out of the ministry mainstream. There they join other members who because of health, conflict, or burn-out pressures are also fringe members.

Here's a hint of hope for churches and leaders: Some fringe members serve as variance sensors.[6] They are usually members who have been formerly active and have participated in the congregation for a time. At present they are still loyal to the church, but they serve only as passive observers of the church's life. They understand the dream of the congregation and can sense when the direction of the church is at variance from the dream. They see more potential and want more attention to kingdom dreams and ministries than others.

Variance sensors are valuable resources for church leaders. These loyal members aren't ready to re-enlist in the fray, but when approached will usually offer perspective, counsel, and encouragement to leaders who are trying to facilitate the dreaming process. Variance sensors make observations from behind the scenes, but they aren't yet willing to accept leadership responsibility again. They offer informal guidance, but even informal suggestions from persons who understand the difference between dreaming and drifting make leaders wiser.

I learned from a variance sensor in a former church who offered wise advice—that is, when I asked for his guidance. We played golf together most Thursdays, and I took a "research question" about the church with me on each trip to the golf course. I'd ask my question on the tee. Since we usually sliced and hooked the golf ball in different directions, he had time to think about my inquiry before we met again on the next green. I'd ask, he'd think, he'd answer, and I'd learn. His insights guided me well.

Conflict often leaves the congregation's visionaries inactive or ready to exit.[7] It's possible for much of the spiritual strength of a church to be left in an observer's role after a church fight. Leaders don't ignore the edges or margins of their organizations. And, they don't lose the zeal of their calling.

Prophets on the Fringe

Although some members on the fringe of a congregation may not have lost their personal calling or negated their church's dream, others can be deadly to the dream. When congregations slide into unhealthy patterns, "reluctant prophets" come to church. These types remember better days, raise questions, stir doubts, disagree deeply, move to the fringes of ministry, and sometimes drop out completely. This declining side of the health cycle is evident in the Old Testament story of Jonah.

Jonah was a classic reluctant prophet. His story contrasts the spread of religious disease with faith's discovery. God called Jonah to prophesy to Nineveh, a city in great spiritual need. God's redemptive dream for the prophet and the city were clear, strong, and enduring.

Jonah missed the message, though. He was nostalgic for the old days before the Exile. Emotionally committed to an era before Nineveh was Israel's enemy, Jonah ran from God rather than preach to a foe. Questioning God, Jonah boarded a ship sailing in the opposite direction from Nineveh and went below deck. Already feeling safe and free, he settled in for a nap. He thought he had left God's call in his rearview mirror.

One of the ironies of unhealthy churches and their "prophets" is that outsiders may pray and act with more piety than those inside the congregations. When severe storms threatened Jonah's ship, the worried crew prayed for deliverance and readied themselves to discard burdensome cargo. The increasingly frantic sailors finally awakened Jonah and invited him to pray with them for deliverance. Then, they remembered he had already told them he was fleeing from God. Soon they discerned that Jonah was the actual object of the storm's wrath. When the sea raged even more, as a last resort, they threw Jonah overboard along with extra cargo. The sea calmed immediately, and the relieved crew gratefully worshipped the Creator God with sacrifices and new vows. Oddly, Jonah's absence made his first converts.

God wasn't through with a reluctant Jonah. From a fish's stomach, Jonah got spit up on his home beach. His call from God still in force, Jonah felt torn and polarized in his heart. Nineveh remained his enemy. In his view the evil city was unworthy of God's grace and mercy. With continuing reservations, Jonah washed the fish saliva off and went to Nineveh. There he preached the Bible's shortest sermon—only eight words: "Yet 40 days, and Nineveh will be overthrown" (Jonah 3:4). With his job finally and minimally done, Jonah stepped back and waited for God's fire to fall on the city.

To the reluctant prophet's great surprise and chagrin, the city repented. From the king to the cows, brokenness reigned. The city was spared from the vengeance Jonah wanted and expected.

An angry Jonah pouted and railed at God for his mercy. He dropped out. He begged God to let him die. Twice, God asked Jonah why he was so angry. Jonah had no answers.

In contrast to Nineveh's new acceptance of God, Jonah's old anger hadn't cooled as the story's record closed. Even in the face of miraculous change in Nineveh, Jonah never discovered the true and larger nature of God. The short prophetic book ends with Jonah still missing that his God was an inclusive redeemer. Jonah couldn't see that God was for everyone, everywhere, on every day.

Jonah's theological blindness is too common when health wanes and congregational conflict—internal and external—reigns. "We are first and God's best" displays a deadly attitude. Reluctant prophets rarely dream again.

The Health Hope

Jesus' kingdom stories expand our view of God and God's reach. The parables invite readers and hearers to discover the depths of God's love and inclusion. These redemptive stories make John's point that God sacrificially loved and continues to love the entire world (John 3:16).

The hope? For congregations to see the depth of God's love and dream again. It's the only way back to health and vitality.

Notes

[1] The chapter title comes from the Apostles' Creed: "He descended into hell."

[2] Edgar H. Schein, *Process Consultation* (Reading, MA: Addison-Wesley, 1969), 18.

[3] Rosabeth Moss Kanter and Barry A. Stein, eds., *Life in Organizations: Workplaces as People Experience Them* (New York: Basic Books, 1979), 377.

[4] Speed Leas and Paul Kittlaus, *Church Fights: Managing Conflict in the Local Church* (Philadelphia: Westminster, 1973), 43-48.

[5] "Looking from the Inside Out," *Time*, 3 October 1977, 85.

[6] Warren Bennis, *The Unconscious Conspiracy: Why Leaders Can't Lead* (New York: AMACOM, 1976), 63. Another type of variance sensor is the active member who is a good problem identifier. This type of person is generally under fire from other members who prefer to avoid problems and think positively all the time.

[7] Stephen Brewster, "Why Your Best Leaders Leave Your Church," http://churchleaders.com/pastors/pastor-articles/303967-best-leaders-leave-church-stephen-brewster, 19 May 2017.

PART 4

Cultivating a
Healthy Dream

Chapter 10

Dreaming Again: Covenant and Cases

It has been observed that over time, institutions move in a predictable sequence: from a man (or woman) to a movement to a machine to a monument.

Organizations emerge out of their original dreams, depend on their visionaries, and show more energy when they're new. The second generation and later institutional leaders inherit more complexity and often place less emphasis on the founding dream than founders. The movement loses momentum and ossifies a bit. Then, leaders settle for oiling the machine and maintaining the monument.

Or, congregations dream again. Healthy futures call for discernment and deliberate decisions—for redreaming. Some congregations slide into the deadly pattern of maintaining themselves and simply surviving. Wise churches return to basics by dreaming and planning, their healthier options.

This chapter suggests some ways the dreaming and redreaming process can be implemented. Let's begin with an actual case, the young Lakeside Church.

Good Storm or Bad Storm?

Lakeside Church grew from a healthy and happy history. At five years old the congregation numbered nearly 600 members. Located in a planned city on a South Carolina lake, the community residents around Lakeside Church are mostly Protestant, middle-aged, and financially successful. But not all was well with the congregation.

The birth of Lakeside Church emerged from providing worship experiences for persons living in the growing housing development. Two couples organized an Easter worship service. The pastor of a nearby church preached. More than 200 persons gathered around tables on a terrace overlooking the water. That level of interest and participation opened a door of opportunity.

The first Easter service, a success, concluded with an announcement. Three days later more than two dozen people met and explored the possibility of starting a church. They organized a steering committee of five men and six women to arrange worship services for a four-month trial period. Informally, several key actions quickly occurred.

First, a donation led to opening a bank account. And, someone loaned a portable organ to the committee. All 61 families who lived in the Lakeside development at that time received news by telephone about the plans for future worship services. A polling of Lakeside's residents showed keen interest in a church, including both Bible study and worship.

After the trial period of worship services concluded successfully in August, the budding congregation took a formal step. They elected co-moderators to lead them. Worship continued, and discussion about developing a Sunday School and budget began. A steering committee also began looking for a building site. The dream was taking hold.

In October the group organized a Sunday School. Christmas Eve saw a high experience of worship, setting a precedent. Easter and Christmas Eve continue to be special times of worship at Lakeside.

The growing group outlined some plans for calling a pastor. But the little church had outgrown itself and needed to be "re-potted." During the spring the growing church wilted a bit because of disorganization. Leaders called in a consultant to help the steering committee develop some specific plans. These plans yielded another significant step. In August a pastor selection committee was formed and immediately began searching for a full-time minister.

A Covenant for Charter Members

In the providence of God, a young minister in North Carolina was dreaming of a church such as Lakeside. By December the search committee and the young minister had met, talked, and arranged a trial sermon. During the initial sermon the prospective pastor used an illustration about a storm. As if on cue, a storm blew across the lake at that very moment. After the sermon the search committee humorously told the young minister that no one would dare vote against him after he called a storm in with exquisite timing! The call vote was strongly affirmative. In May, Lakeside had its first full-time pastor on the ministry field.

The pastor immediately began a series of sermons and discussions to clarify the theological roots of this emerging congregation. One doctrinal position remained central: Jesus Christ is Lord of all of life. Additionally, the concept of the church centered on two ideas: the church gathered for worship and renewal, and the church scattered for mission and ministry.

These sermons produced two important results. One, a covenant of the faith and dream of this group emerged. The covenant (below), accepted by the congregation in September, beautifully affirmed the corporate beliefs of the group.

> We believe in God the Father, Creator and creative,
>   He gives us his steadfast love,
>   shares with us our joy,
>   and sustains us in our suffering.
>   His power is open to us. We trust him.
> We follow Jesus Christ, Son of God and Son of Man.
>   His death becomes our victory,
>   His resurrection is our hope.
> In him the Word has become flesh.
>   In him we are offered
>   forgiveness from sin,
>   renewal from failure,
>   reconciliation from brokenness,
>   release from despair.
> We are guided by the Holy Spirit, God's presence in the world.
>   By the Spirit we are called into Christ's church:
>   to celebrate his love,
>   to see justice and resist evil.
>   To proclaim Jesus, crucified and risen,
>   to share him in baptism and eat at his table.

Because we are his disciples, his pilgrim people, we joyfully
covenant with each other
to walk together in love,
to pray for one another,
to care for one another,
to live in *koinonia*.
In life, in death, in life beyond death
God is with us.
We are not alone.
Thanks be to God!
Amen.[1]

Two, using the covenant as the congregation's defining dream, a call
was issued for charter members. In October, 150 Christians declared
their faith, and Lakeside Church became a reality after several months of
worshiping together. The dream had come true. Or, had it?

Two events upset the congregation. First, a fire wiped out the congregation's office and Sunday School space. Second, the search for a permanent
building site was met with repeated frustration.

Finally, the congregation purchased a new site and took bids on con-
struction, with groundbreaking in August. In May of the next year, the
third year of their life together, the congregation dedicated a new multiuse
facility.

The Future Unfolds

During the next two and a half years, success followed success. The congregation grew to more than 550 members. Worship, music, drama, study, and
outreach ministries flourished.

Growth, however, brought its own looming specter. The new members
did not understand the dream fully, and some longer-term members forgot
their founding dream. Frustration began to simmer.

Fortunately, the minister read his congregation correctly and wisely.
Even with only six years of life together, this congregation showed early
signs of beginning to plateau and tilting toward nostalgia. The minister
devised a year-long, seven-event plan to redream the dream.

Product

Billing address

Richard Poindexter
125 Currituck Ln
Durham, NC 27703
 704-533-3230

✉ richard.poindexter@gmail.com

Product Categories

1. A four-month period recalled the **mileposts** in Lakeside's faith journey. Members remembered and reported, through testimonies in worship, the early stages of Lakeside's dream.

2. A **sermon series on the doctrine of the church** in the congregation's covenant supplied both a biblical review for older members and an orientation for newer ones.

3. A **welcome program** for new members focused on two challenges: making the congregational dream clearer and making the church's ministries easier to join.

4. At a two-week **Christian festival of the arts**, more than 200 members shared their creative gifts through music, painting, drama, and puppetry. Members became better acquainted, and fellowship was strengthened.

5. The missions committee involved a larger number of members in **direct ministry and outreach**, resulting in four new projects that extended the reach of the congregation.

6. Four **sermons on the parables**, coupled with four **dramatic presentations** on specific parables, awakened the hearers to Jesus' kingdom dream. The tension between service and "serve us" was spotlighted.

7. Fifty adult church members, including most of the church council and committee chairpersons, met at an area **retreat** center to evaluate the church's purpose and progress. Broader ownership of the kingdom dream resulted.

Was reawakening the dream worth the effort for Lakeside? Yes. A difference became obvious in the life and work of the congregation. The two months following the completion of these seven events of discernment and discovery saw a new growth spurt with 100 new members joining. The pastor sensed a new focus in his own ministry. Congregational morale heightened.

Lakeside's dream anchored and unified the congregation again. The members had redreamed their dream and were ready to look toward God's redemptive work in their future.

Approaches for Dreaming Again

Without attempting an exhaustive overview of all possible dreaming strategies, let's identify some more common approaches for dreaming again at
three levels of congregational life. We'll explore gatherings of the entire
congregation, the work of smaller groups, and the initiative of leaders.

Proclaiming the Dream Publicly

Some aspects of awakening a dream fit total congregational settings. Worship
is the most obvious public arena for proclaiming the dream and raising the
consciousness of the entire congregation. Sermons, testimonies, and other
types of presentations can define and undergird a congregation's health cycle.

For example, *sermons* on the parables extend the dreaming process and
show how contemporary congregations become "like the kingdom." For
example, the precious pearl parable (Matt. 13:45-46) illustrates the dimension of sacrifice and risk inherent when we become like the kingdom. Again,
the mustard seed parable (Matt. 13:31-32) shows the potential of kingdom
growth in its small-to-large contrast. Sermons built around the various stages
of the health cycle also strengthen a congregation's dream, for example:

- A cluster of sermons on the parables explores and undergirds the
  dream stage. In media-savvy churches, phone apps are now being used by
  preachers to poll or interact with the congregation during sermons. Then,
  preaching about the congregation's dream becomes more of a conversation about church health and possible futures.

- Anchoring the **beliefs stage** takes lots of shapes. Lakeside Church wrote
  its own covenant. Beliefs also are solidified by taking selected favorite
  congregational hymns that undergird the dream and building worship
  experiences around them.

- The **goals stage** focuses sermons and conversations on "Jesus Helped
  Others." Since goals grow out of beliefs and dreams, show how Jesus'
  kingdom dream expressed itself concretely in specific ministry events.

- The "Shape of the Early Church," a sermon series on the Pastoral Epistles, illustrates the **structure stage**. The Pastorals give clues about the way the first congregations structured their lives to implement the kingdom dream.

- The **ministry stage** might focus on Acts, especially the range of mission and ministry actions the emerging church took to extend its ministry. Evangelism, fellowship, nurture, benevolence, confronting cultural barriers, and global outreach—a few concrete ministry elements—demonstrate the diversity of the church of Acts in its practice of ministry. The series might arrange itself around the theme, "Scattered to Embody Christ."

- "Temptations to Turn Back" explore the **nostalgia stage**. The post-Exodus wilderness wanderings and the "early retirement" of the Thessalonian Christians suggest themes to illustrate how nostalgia short-circuits ministry energies.

Obviously, brief series of sermons would focus members' attention on congregational health concerns for an extended time. As much as a year, excluding seasonal themes and special issues, might be needed in this approach. Ministers and other leaders determine if an effort of this magnitude is a project they want to undertake.

In addition to sermons, *lay testimonies* in worship give individual members a way to express their dream for the congregation. In worship settings visionary laypersons share their current and future dreams for their congregation. To maintain focus, they may be asked to complete this sentence: "Five years from now, I hope our church will be . . . " These testimonies, woven into ordinary worship services, become vision-stretching exercises. Or, a larger portion of a service can focus on impromptu testimonies with the intent of showing the breadth of vision in a church. In either case, the focus stays on the future and on enlarging concrete ministry actions implied by the dream.

Supporting the Dream

Congregations, made up of teaching-learning classes and small groups, use those gatherings to clarify dreams and develop consensus. Small clusters of members lend themselves well to personal encouragement and congregational health purposes. A range of possibilities fits small groups.

- If small groups provide educational settings, Jesus' parables can be studied together. To prepare for teaching the parables and to lead discussion, ask yourself these four interpretive questions:

  1. What's the main point of this parable?
  2. Who is being addressed and under what circumstances?
  3. What comparisons and/or contrasts emerge?
  4. What must I do now as a faith response to this parable?

  The parables create tensions in their comparisons and contrasts that help define and focus a kingdom dream. Look at the challenges in Jesus' high-profile stories:

  –Old and New (Luke 5:36-39)
  –Small and Large (Luke 13:18-21)
  –Festivity and Faithfulness (Matt. 22:1-14)
  –Planning and Piety (Luke 14:28-33)
  –Lost and Found (Luke 15)
  –Neighbor Need and Christian Care (Luke 10:29-37)
  –Riches and Rewards (Luke 16:19-31)
  –Prayers and Parade (Luke 18:9-14)

- A theological focus on God's kingdom and congregational life offers study and discussion options for small groups. Again, such a study concentrates on how the body of Christ lives out its kingdom dream.

- Exploring our own spiritual roots provides an anchoring process. For example, each person in a small group draws and shares his or her spiritual family tree. This drawing traces individual spiritual heritage. With a facilitator, a second stage of mapping spiritual pilgrimages develops a composite family tree for the congregation at large. Such an interpretive document helps groups in two ways: to examine the spiritual roots that nourish their corporate dream and to grow new branches on the family tree.

Deepening Commitment to the Dream

Leaders of any enterprise need clarity about and commitment to their purposes. As leaders become clearer about shared dreams, they commit themselves more deeply to those dreams. The ministers and elected leaders of church groups may design planning retreats to examine the congregation's dream.

The Hillwood Church used a simple approach for gathering members' opinions on ministries and programs. The staff asked members to offer their perspectives on two questions:

• What were the highs and lows of last year's ministries?
• What are your hopes and fears for next year's ministries?

Finally, the leadership posted these highs-and-lows along with the now-and-then in four quadrants on large charts headed "Last Year" and "Next Year." This visual comparison showed how members felt about the congregation's progress toward their dream, and thereby made discussion easy.

Also using the members' reports, Hillwood's staff proposed a theme or motto for the next year. For example, the themes for three years indicate their sense of progress: "Let's Turn Things Around," "Growing Up in Every Way," and "Let Us Go On." These mottoes gave the leader group a shorthand way to express their dream and to refocus on it.

Old First Church used a series of Sunday evenings for congregational "town meetings." The first two sessions centered on dreaming about many possibilities. (Electronic "town meetings" and social media had previously pooled options to be explored in public gatherings.) After numerous specific interests began to revolve around the core dream, discussion groups formed around these issues. These 10 or 15 groups suggested ministry possibilities that were then taken to the entire congregation for conversation, discernment, decision, and implementation.

Dare to Dream

Methods vary for awakening a dream, but one dynamic remains constant: Vision is the watershed in healthy congregations.

Edward Lindaman, team leader for America's first moon shot and a Presbyterian lay leader, encouraged us to dream: "It helps to realize that *everything that is now possible was at one time impossible.* In every case someone somewhere dared to dream, dared to imagine something a little better, a little different."[2]

A dream defined and owned can change your church, and ultimately our generation and the world.

Notes

¹Gene Jester, *"Building a Church from a Dream,"* (D.Min. project report, Southeastern Baptist Theological Seminary, 1980), 103.

²Edward B. Lindaman, *Thinking in the Future Tense* (Nashville: Broadman, 1978), 44

Chapter 11

Spurring Vitality: Planning and Leading

"Ninety percent of baseball is mental. The other half is physical." Or, so Yogi Berra, the famed New York Yankee catcher, once observed. Yogi's math was a bit generous, but his statement accurately describes dreaming and planning.

A kingdom-of-God dream, that "90 percent portion" of spiritual and mental success, comes first and requires wisdom and effort. The "other half" of the revitalization process involves planning and implementing, the physical and practical work of ministry.

After the dream roots itself clearly, leaders move toward the kingdom's horizon. We look for new ways to plant, cultivate, and grow. Taken together, dreaming and planning spur new vitality, and the viral impact of dreaming and planning multiplies to more than 100 percent.

As we approach the conclusion of the redreaming process, we have better answers. In the two final chapters of this book we'll answer three foundational questions to bring new vitality to congregational life and ministry:

1. How do we dream for God's kingdom?
2. How do we plan for God's kingdom?
3. How do we lead for God's kingdom?

In chapter 10 we discussed the realm of dreaming for God's kingdom. In this chapter we'll respond to questions related to planning and leading for God's kingdom. Then, we'll put the last pieces of the puzzle to together.

Planning

Congregational planning describes the actions taken to move from dreaming about God's kingdom to doing God's ministry. The essential movements of a planning process can be diagrammed as follows:

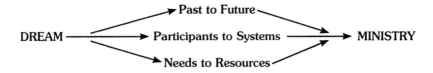

Unlike mechanical methods, planning generates dynamic movement. It creates the crucial link between vision and implementation.

Foundations, Futures, and Faces

Redreaming goes back to basics, while still looking ahead for breakthroughs. These new plans build on the foundation of God's kingdom, look toward future opportunities, and put real faces on ministry challenges. God's kingdom roots churches as they dream again. Cosmetic changes are worthless. Is it time for a deep, courageous reset in your church?

Planning for new dreams calls for speed and finesse, focus and direction. In earlier eras with more stability, goals tended to be sacred, became set in stone, were implemented in lockstep, and could never be adjusted.

Redreaming in our fast-changing world takes lots of imagination, adaptability, and faith. Some leadership theorists preach that internal disruption generates change. That's true enough, but the current pace of change already produces enough outside disruption to stir most churches. Can we stay creative enough to incorporate new discoveries amid massive transition?[1]

Facing constantly changing frontiers, planning becomes an emergent and agile process. For churches, planning is changing in at least two major ways:

1. **Shortened timeframes for planning**—Rather than planning for time horizons of a decade or for several years as in earlier eras, most current planning only looks downstream a few years. In fact, some churches now have permanent groups of planners, making planning an ongoing process instead of an episode.

2. **Increasing flexibility in implementation**—The older lock-step approach to planning is now making room for adaptability. Amid changes, adjustments in ministry directions and goals are triggered by unanticipated events—surprises, new opportunities, and major barriers.

Let's examine some key movements in congregational planning in more detail.

Hope in Action

Theologically, planning is hope in action. Full of hope, planning for kingdom ministry-on-the-move involves seven basic faith steps into God's futures:

1. **Move from continuity to pivot points**—Planning in today's chaotic world doesn't assume step-by-step continuity. Rather, change builds on pivot points, those tips and turns that begin fresh journeys.[2] Pivot points sharpen directions, refocus actions, and provide reminders to seize every new opportunity to advance.

2. **Move from anticipation to action**—It's time to change direction, face disruptions, and wrestle with some key questions:
   • What's changing or accelerating already?
   • How can we respond early, especially to callings that others don't yet have eyes to see?
   • Who are the "future faces" of our congregation?
   • How can we create a redemptive context for these new issues and persons?
   • Where are heavenly, neighborly ministries already peeking through?
   • Redreaming ministry, never theoretical, brings heaven to earth.

3. **Move from present to future**—Planning links today to tomorrow. We can't change our pasts, but yesterday provides us with launch pads for our tomorrows. The future forces congregations to anticipate. Church leaders become futurists, finding God's future before the world shapes us. We choose our preferred future based on the kingdom dream, and then take action.

4. **Move from individuals to systems**—Planning links the energies of individual members to the actions or goals of the entire congregation. Effective planning weaves scattered interests into team ministries. We support what we help create. Ideas developed by a few members are then usually implemented by only a few. Plans made by a broad cross-section of a congregation's members are more apt to become system-wide ministries. The old proverb, "The more, the merrier" applies to participation in church planning.

5. **Move from inside to outside**—Effective planning in a fast-moving era keeps the focus on emerging ministry needs. We're called to care for others. Diverse people groups and human needs beyond the congregation itself stir hearts and hands to reach out. It's not enough for congregations to be happy with ourselves. The kingdom of God calls us to minister to the "least of these," practice neighborliness, and tilt our calendars toward eternity.

6. **Move from generic to distinctive**—Churches with kingdom dreams don't settle for being average or copying other congregations. Dreaming churches seek extraordinary ministries, redemptive service, renewed enthusiasm, and spiritual roots. As organic leaders, we know we can't rush ministries that need time to grow to maturity.

7. **Move from needs to resources**—Planning mediates the movement from the push of human need to the pull of congregational resources. Needs and resources are matched and balanced in planning. Finding that creative intersection is part of the genius of planning.

Hope for the Future

Paul spotlighted faith, hope, and love (1 Cor. 13:13) as foundational for Christian living. Planning frequently energizes hope to create futures for love and faith.

Hope never loses its realism. Hope knows we often fail, and we learn from those stumbles. After all, we fall about 700 times while learning to walk. In fact, the mechanics of walking incorporate controlled falling, but without losing hope.

Brené Brown notes, "Hope is brokenhearted on the way to becoming wholehearted. Hope is a function of struggle."[3] Even with perfect planning, don't expect automatic, immediate victories. Let hope and wisdom flow from failing with grace. Keep on keeping on. Christ embodies our hope (1 Tim. 1:1).

Planning is proactive and healthy, the polar opposite of reactive problem solving. When planning is seen as forward movement, we're reminded that planners have the lever of initiative in their hands. The dreamers provide motivation and horsepower. Planners identify our directions and guide our futures.

Let's explore two dimensions of planning—assessing needs and evaluating resources—more carefully now.

Needs Assessment

Needs, in and beyond the congregation, give church planners a starting line. The movement from opportunities to resources is an especially important planning dynamic. Where are the new opportunities, the opening doors, and the emerging needs for kingdom ministry?

Needs assessment—internal and external to the congregation—forms a base line for planning. Opportunities invite us to plan for them.

Considerable information is available to help congregations profile the external needs of their community and their ministry "draw area." Demographic profiles from census data, municipal and public school planning agencies, and community development groups provide information on what a community is like and what it needs. For example, census data show the age groupings of a neighborhood and offer a clue to whether child care or senior adult ministries fit most appropriately in congregational outreach.

A psychohistory profile provides a tool to make churches more aware of the internal needs of its own members. Such a profile isolates some typical life issues along age-grouping lines. Clusters of age groupings allow us to target promising arenas for ministry.

Six issues illustrate the broad-based needs revealed by a congregational psychohistory profile, as shown in the following chart:

ISSUES

AGES		Religious Needs	Developmental Needs	Family Needs	Vocational Needs
	13-20	Developing a sense of belonging. Establishing a personal, independent faith.	Learning one's identity or identity diffusion, to be an independent, faithful, sexual, career person.	Crucial importance of peer group.	Tentative choice of a lifework. Part-time jobs give taste of work world.
	18-35	Stabilizing deep relationships. Growing a faith sturdy enough for adulthood, family, and professional demands.	Learning to achieve intimacy or isolation, to love, to make commitments to others without losing oneself.	Selecting a spouse or choosing singleness. Adjusting to marriage. Child bearing. Family is focus of some wives. Threat of divorce.	Vocational moratorium. Work is focus of husband and wife. Search for mentors. Commit to a career.
	35-55	Discovering a sense of self-renewal. Creating a clear focus for living.	Learning to generate or be self-absorbed, to create, to develop new challenges.	Child rearing. Child launching. Wife's career. Returning father. Switch-40s.	Becoming one's own person. Becoming a mentor. Risking new career ventures.
	55-up	Finding a sense of satisfaction, meaning, and purpose. Trusting the future to God and younger generations.	Learning to feel integrity or disgust and despair, to discover, to transfer hope to others, to face aging, fixed income, and death.	Empty nest. Retirement adjustments. Single partner after spouse's death.	Moving from leadership to followership. Retirement. Second career.

ACTION EXERCISE #12

Discovering Generational Needs

- What percentage of our congregation fits into each age group?
- What are the three largest age groups?
- What are the special needs and concerns of these largest age groups?
- What is our church providing currently to minister to these special needs? What else could be provided?
- What are the unique strengths of these largest age groups that can be used as ministry resources?
- What age group is missing from our congregation?

Strong ministry to strategic needs helps a congregation minister effectively and appropriately. A psychohistory profile of your church helps you focus on key ministry issues with more awareness and confidence. Healthy ministry grows from planning to meet real needs.

Remember that missing groups have needs too. What would it take for your congregation to reach out to these missing groups? If reaching other groups is in your church's future, how do you prepare for and provide for these people and their needs?

Resources Evaluation

Resources are basic to planning. Any church has a range of resources: members' energy, buildings and property, offerings and savings, community influence, and information. Human resources, though, are the most important of all. Without people, a congregation ceases to exist.

The health cycle model lends itself to evaluating human resources. Each stage of the cycle has church members who seem to relate to and take ownership of that stage most naturally. Assigning persons to each of the nine stages offers a subjective picture of a congregation's human resources. (This is a behind-the-scenes beginning to resource discovery and is to be kept confidential since most of us don't want to be labeled in public.)

Start by making nine lists of members' names. Head these lists with general titles:

1. "Visionaries" (for the dream)
2. "Theologians" (for beliefs)
3. "Explorers" (of goals)
4. "Organizers" (for structure)
5. "Activists" (for ministry)
6. "Traditionalists" (for nostalgia)
7. "Detectives" (for questioning)
8. "Fighters" (during polarization)
9. "Apathetics" (during drop-out)

Then, place each person's name on the list in the grouping that seems to be her best overall designation at the present.

Persons included in the first six lists indicate those who will minister with you. They are your congregation's most positive human resources. Even the Traditionalists are valuable for your congregation's future, because they can signal when organization slippage is beginning.

Within the first six lists, note the longer lists. They represent your congregation's primary "people strengths" for ministry. The longer lists name the members who make your church productive. On the other hand, any shorter lists between "Visionaries" to "Traditionalists" indicate a training and development need. Shorter lists show you where to concentrate recruitment and training efforts.

ACTION EXERCISE #13
Human Resource Survey

• Who are our congregation's visionaries? Theologians? Explorers? Organizers? Activists? Traditionalists? Detectives? Fighters? Apathetics?
• What are the largest groups? What do they signify? What do they provide our congregation?
• What are the smallest groups? What do they signify? What do they provide our congregation?
• Overall, how would you describe the human resource and training picture in our church? What plans are appropriate now?

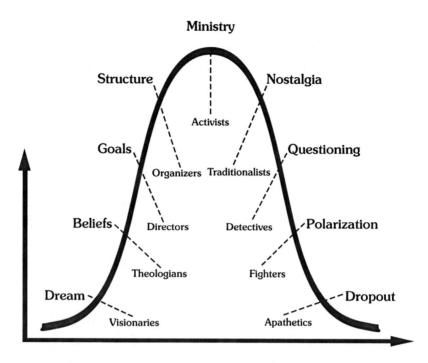

The final three lists—Detectives, Fighters, and Apathetics—identify members who need the ministry of their own congregation. Longer lists here aren't assets. Neither do shorter lists necessarily indicate trainable persons. Healthy congregations will tend to have shorter lists in these final three categories. The basic signal from the final three groups is simple: Minister to us first or we are unlikely to join you in ministry to others again.

Congregational planners also need to give attention to new members. New members assume they know their new church's dream; long-term members assume the dream is obvious. Those two assumptions, when left unexamined, can begin an erosion of the dream.

Picture the challenge like this: Visualize each stage of the health cycle as a door to your congregation. Potentially, a new member enters your church through any of these doors. For example, a new member identifies with a specific goal, such as increasing Sunday School attendance or starting a ministry to the deaf, and he enters through that goal door. Or, the goal could be a nostalgic identification with a building or a minister, evoking memories from the past. So, the new member joins your church through that door and doesn't see how his favorite goal or ministry or memory connects to the dream.

Quite unintentionally, he helps dissipate the congregation's resources. Why? Because he has no concept of the core dream from which goals or ministries grew. A kingdom dream is the glue that connects and holds the entire congregation together.

A new member orientation process tailored to each congregation's special dream provides a solution to the doors issue. Most new member orientation programs major on what time the Sunday School meets or where to find the choir rehearsal room or some key doctrinal distinctive. These items are needed, but the healthiest beginning point is the dream itself. New members need to discover how their church's dream came to life and how it has been lived out. Then, using the dream as an anchor, the elements of ministry, education, missions, and music fit in.

High Hills Church followed this design in its new member orientation program. Several times each year on three consecutive Sunday evenings, church leaders conduct two-hour sessions organized along these lines:

• Session 1 centers on the kingdom dream of High Hills Church. Testimonies of long-term members and visual presentations guide new members through an overview of the unique development of this congregation.

• Session 2 focuses on the inward journey of the dream. Worship, Bible study, and retreats are some of High Hills' resources to stimulate spiritual growth.

• Session 3 pivots toward the outward journey of witness, mission, and community ministries. In fact, one mission support group guides High Hills' new member orientation process. By helping new members discover their congregation's dream, this mission support group finds the doors to both the journey inward and journey outward easier to open for newcomers.

Dreams are roots for plans. Plans are fruit from dreams. Planning is the preventive and proactive leader skill behind congregational health. Whether your church is an Old First, a growing suburban one, or a rural family chapel, the process is basic. Dreaming and planning are teamed creatively in and for congregational health.

Dreams without plans are fantasies. Plans without dreams are adrift. A dream and a plan support congregational health. Our plans translate our kingdom dream into concrete ministry. And, our leadership community, the not-so-secret sauce in that church's health recipe, makes the difference.

Leading

Jesus' first recorded leadership event was the wedding feast at Cana (John 2:1-11). Notice the different ways Jesus led: in the center of the group, on the edges of the group, and between subgroups. Perhaps relatives of the bride or groom, he and his mother were likely in the middle of the multi-day celebration. We see him on the edge of the group when his mother reported a wine shortage. And, we also see him interacting across the group.

Leaders influence congregational transformation in the same ways—in centers, on edges, and to subgroups.[4]

Relating to the Whole System

Teamed together, leaders multiply impacts by moving fluidly across the entire church system and cultivating productive relationships in all arenas of the congregation. Leaders live and serve in the center and on the congregation's edges and bridge between groups in the church and groups beyond the church.

- As **center leaders**, we immerse ourselves in the core life of the church. We serve our congregation's present and future. We dream, pray, teach, witness, visit, welcome, and generally lubricate the entire atmosphere of the church. Center leaders are the faces of the dream.

- As **edge leaders**, we're scouts and sentries on the rim of the congregation. Objectively, we look inward to see strengths, fill gaps, and encourage emerging leaders within the church. We advocate for what we have eyes to see. With anticipation, we look outward and beyond our church's current life. We are first to see the next challenges our congregation will face and the next opportunities we can pursue. We're eyes for the congregation's dream.

- As **bridge leaders**, we are internal and external link persons for the congregation. We move with ease across the church's subgroups, keeping others involved and informed. We also are the relational bridges with community partners and to outside resources, moving across traditional boundaries. We open conversations and keep them flowing. We form connections and cultivate them. We're hands and feet for the dream.

Leaders dream and plan, discern and discover. Congregational leaders serve the church's futures, multiplying themselves and making a difference, reaching out and growing.

Responding to Tensions

Today's leaders face "grow or else" tensions as we dream and plan. Like rubber bands, we are kept stretched to the maximum by our challenges and opportunities. Let's explore three of those ongoing pressures from talent, teams, and time.[5]

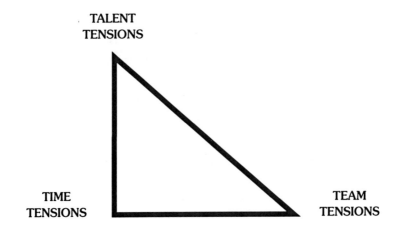

TALENT
TENSIONS

TIME
TENSIONS

TEAM
TENSIONS

- **Talent tensions** revolve around inside-outside stretches. While leaders often are stretched to find ways to use the full array of gifts and strengths we have inside our congregations, we also know that God's kingdom calls for more talent than we may currently have on the inside. That realization refocuses us to reach for some outside resources. We then begin to renew our inside leader corps, grow new leaders to bridge the inside-outside gaps, and look for outside ministry partners. Talent tensions require spanning and stretching.

- **Team tensions** revolve around ability-agility stretches. Leaders multiply group abilities by identifying gifts, expanding knowledge, and providing safe environments for new leaders to grow and take risks. But that's not enough. We live in a speeding world, one that changes without warning. So, leaders cultivate team agility, adaptability, and new capacities for making decisions amid constant chaos. Today's leaders face a world brimming with possibilities, uncertain circumstances, and increasingly shorter time-frames. Team tensions require hoping and stretching.

- **Time tensions** revolve around now-then stretches. Leaders understand that ministry effectiveness bridges today and tomorrow. Clear-eyed leaders have both bifocal and distance vision. In our churches we see those ministries that have already run their course and those opportunities that are barely beginning to emerge. We constantly build on our congregation's healthiest DNA as we search for our best futures. We don't rest on our laurels; we peer over horizons to anticipate where God has already prepared paths for us. Time tensions require "futuring" and stretching.

To be stretched without snapping and to respond creatively to our tensions are growing edges for today's leaders. It's our moment to grow, serve, and make a kingdom difference.

Our Opportunity, Our Moment

Ready for your leadership moment? Dream and plan. Lead and make a difference. Serve God's kingdom so heaven comes on earth. That's our call. We have God's blessing to live it out now.

You've used *To Dream Again, Again!* and its "action exercises" as a self-guided tour of your church and its health profile. You've seen some new dynamics in your church and understand them better. You've become a better and healthier leader. That may be all you need to support your congregation's kingdom dream. If so, may God bless you and your church now and into the future. But maybe you need more help to dream again.

Is it time to invite a consultant to walk with your congregation on its pilgrimage to health and vitality? If so, read the epilogue and act now.

Notes

[1]Gareth Morgan, *Imaginization: New Mindsets for Seeing, Organizing, and Managing* (San Francisco: Berrett-Koehler, 1997), 41-61.

[2]David B. Drake, *Narrative Coaching: Bringing Our New Stories to Life* (Petaluma, CA: CNC Press, 2005), 190-208.

[3]Krista Tippett, *Becoming Wise: An Inquiry into the Mystery and Art of Living* (New York: Penguin, 2016), 251.

[4]Bob Dale and Bill Wilson, *Weaving Strong Leaders: How Leaders Grow Down, Grow Up, and Grow Together* (Macon, GA: Nurturing Faith, 2016), 26-27.

[5]David B. Peterson and Mary Dee Hicks, *Leaders as Coaches: Strategies for Coaching and Developing Others* (Minneapolis, MN: Personnel Decisions International Corporation, 1996).

Afterword

Living God's Dream

Mark Zuckerberg, Facebook CEO, laid out his vision for the next frontier of social media. Facebook's updated mission statement is "Bring the world closer together." Zuckerberg foresees online communities replacing churches, Little League, and community support groups.[1] With many younger people leaving traditional congregations behind, could Zuckerberg be right?

Yes and no. All of us need and want community. Lots of groups, real and virtual, supply connections for us to enjoy. But congregations are more than just compatible groups of contacts.

Covenants of care and partners in service provide root systems for our faith communities. Churches, in contrast to secular communities, gather and scatter to incarnate heaven on earth. God's dream, not human interests, makes the distinguishing difference. After all, the kingdom of God defines us.

Thomas Jefferson once hoped that America would have a revolution every 20 years. Jefferson wasn't advocating overthrow of the government. He envisioned no battles, new flags, or prisoners of war. Jefferson wanted a redefining of America for every new generation.

Church health flows from a defined dream of God's kingdom. Congregations either redefine their basic purpose every generation or they die. The road to health and continued vitality is to dream again.

Famed aviator Charles A. Lindbergh stated our hope: "We actually live today in our dreams of yesterday; and, living in these dreams, we dream again."

The good news of Christ's redemptive kingdom hasn't changed for eons. We have only to dream it again.

Note

[1] http://www.cnbc.com/2017/06/26/mark-zuckerberg-compares-facebook-to-church-little-league.html

Epilogue

Helping Your Church to "Dream Again"

By Bill Wilson

More than 30 years ago I found myself serving as pastor of a small church and desperately needing guidance and direction. Enter Bob Dale's classic book, *To Dream Again*. The principles taught in this book transformed my thinking and led to a season of renewed energy, mission, and vision for our congregation. Across the years I have returned again and again to the foundational concepts and practices I first discovered in this epic book.

Some of you who are reading this new edition of Bob's work will find yourself where I did: needing insights and suggestions for how to lead a congregation to redream its sense of godly purpose and direction. You may be able to take the lessons from concept to implementation by yourself. We certainly hope that will be the case. The content in these pages needs to be widely disseminated and shared across your fellowship.

However, most of us who have traveled down this path of congregational health have also encountered times when we have not been objective enough or disengaged enough from our parish or congregation to see clearly what the issues are or what the remedy might be. We are too close, too enmeshed, and too subjective to observe all that needs to be seen. Our plates are full, and we need another set of eyes and hands for this task.

If that is the case with you, please consider inviting the Center for Healthy Churches to come alongside your place of ministry and assist you in a redreaming process. Some of the most important work an external congregational coach/consultant can do is help you frame the right questions and listen fully and without prejudice to the responses. It is a gift to have a guide, or scout, or encourager along for the difficult journey of transformation.

The Center for Healthy Churches is blessed by a team of congregational coaches who share some core convictions about our work:

- We love the local church/parish and believe in it.
- We have had on-the-ground experience and success as leaders in local churches
- We are primarily motivated by our love for the church, and not by financial gain.

Our team members have had experience working in a variety of denominational and congregational settings. Large or small, rural or urban, conservative or progressive, informal or formal, new or old, we have been partners with nearly every type and style of church imaginable. We are ready to help you implement the ideas and principles spelled out in this book.

If you would like to talk with a CHC congregational coach about how we might be of help as you seek to redream the dream of your congregation or parish, please contact us and let us share with you how that might happen.

Center for Healthy Churches
4911 Salem Glen Blvd.
Clemmons, NC 27012
contact@chchurches.org
(336) 970-3578

CPSIA information can be obtained
at www.ICGtesting.com
Printed in the USA
FFOW02n1942030318
45411327-46108FF

9 781635 280296